EMPOWERING WOMEN... As I See

Kiran Bedi

Voted as the Most Admired and Trusted Woman in India by the following media and surveys:

The Most Admired Woman: *The Week,* September 15, 2002.

Among 15 Indian Icons Who Have Made Us Proud: *The Week*, June 6, 2006.

Among Top Five India's Most Trusted Personalities 2009 (and highest ranked woman): Survey by *The Digital Edge* for *Readers Digest*.

The Most Admired Indian Female Icon 2011: *MSN She User's Choice Awards*.

India's Most Trusted Woman Personality: *Trust Research Advisory, Brand Trust Report, India Study, 2013* (second year in a row).

By the same author

As I See (2013)
Empowering Women...As I See (2013)
Dare to Do! For the New Generation (2012)
It's Always Possible (2012)
Be the Change: Fighting Corruption (2012)
I Dare! (2011)
What Went Wrong and Continuous? (2011)

EMPOWERING WOMEN... As I See

Kiran Bedi

STERLING PAPERBACKS
An imprint of
Sterling Publishers (P) Ltd.
A-59, Okhla Industrial Area, Phase-II,
New Delhi-110020.
Tel: 26387070, 26386209; Fax: 91-11-26383788
E-mail: mail@sterlingpublishers.com
www.sterlingpublishers.com

Empowering Women: As I See
© 2013, Kiran Bedi
ISBN 978 81 207 8114 6

All rights are reserved.
No part of this publication may be reproduced, stored in a retrieval system or transmitted, in any form or by any means, mechanical, photocopying, recording or otherwise, without prior written permission of the original publisher.

Printed in India

Printed and Published by Sterling Publishers Pvt. Ltd.,
New Delhi-110 020.

Why this book?

Being a woman is both an asset and a liability. A lot depends on what she makes of herself and what she becomes.

A woman is a huge asset when she is self-dependent and possesses the awareness and choice of being interdependent.

She is a liability when she is neither educated nor financially independent and, worse, when she is psychologically dependent on others for her physical well-being. In such a situation she is truly enslaved. And we have millions of such women all over the world.

These articles are "As I See" the situation. They are each the result of an observation, experience, feeling, and learning. At the same time, they are also expressions of joy and concern. They are about lessons to be learnt.

Wishing you the very best in the times ahead.

Acknowledgements

I am grateful to:

India Vision Foundation staff: Monica Dhawan, Archana Kumar, Lata Kumari, Kundan Singh, Nanda Dass, Nobat Ram, Rajiv Kumar, Ram Prakash, Sumitra Rai, Sunil Gautam, and Tarun Rohilla for their generous support in secretarial management, articles retrieval, and technology support.

Webmaster Anup Sinha for updating the social network and the website www.kiranbedi.com.

Shri Surinder Kumar Ghai, Managing Director, Sterling Publishers (P) Ltd. and his team.

Sanjiv Sarin, the editor of this book.

Contents

	Why this book?	v
	Acknowledgements	vii
1.	Avoid Pitfalls and Blunders in Life	1
2.	Be Yourself—Be Not a Man	5
3.	Blurred, yet Moved	8
4.	Dawn of a New Generation	11
5.	Double Standards	15
6.	Early Marriage: Till the Tears Run Dry	18
7.	Girl Child Education: Duty or Liability?	22
8.	How Can We Be Heard?	26
9.	It's Good to Be a Saheli	29
10.	Know This Law and Prevent Violence	32
11.	Let's Help Ourselves	36
12.	Marriage and Identity Crisis	39
13.	Not Born Free	42
14.	Pregnant Questions	45
15.	To Be Home by Sunset	48
16.	Where Women Groan under Bride Price	52
17.	Woman, Help Her, Help Yourself	55
18.	Do You Really Mean Business?	58
19.	Build Women's Trust in Police	62
20.	First Ladies, Take the Lead	66
21.	Get Up, It's Your World Too!	69
22.	Giving Asia Women Leaders	72
23.	Preventable Pain	75

24.	Women Sarpanch as Rubber Stamps	78
25.	Women, Seize the Day!	81
26.	The Journey to Fearlessness	84
27.	A Bunch of Keys	87
28.	Women Leadership on Test	91
29.	Needed Many More Millions	94
30.	Neutralising Man-Made Imbalances	97
31.	Eating the Elephant	100
32.	Parents like Mine	103
33.	Responsible Parenting	106
34.	Seeing Indian Women in a Time Warp	108
35.	Where There Is a Will There Is a Way	111
36.	Whose Fault?	114
37.	Use Education as a Key to Empowerment	117
38.	Soft Backbones and Hard Hearts	120
39.	Whoever and Wherever	124
40.	Taking Care of Women in Distress	128
41.	Are They Pretty Pageants or Beauty Contests?	131
42.	Danger Zone: Men and Women at Work	134
43.	Will They Listen to Me?	137
44.	Women in Uniform: Who Are They?	141
45.	Unjust God?	145
46.	India's Emerging Face	148
47.	National Rainbows	151
48.	Two Interesting Experiences	155
49.	No Short Cuts	158
50.	Questions Which Need Answers	162
51.	Women as Catalysts for Transformation	165
52.	Women—Educated but Still Disempowered	168

1
Avoid Pitfalls and Blunders in Life

While on a visit to a school to attend its Foundation day function in Bhubaneshwar, Odisha, I was informed that there was an engineering college for women on the way and the students were very keen to have an interaction with me. Fortunately, my flight back to Delhi was delayed and I had the time. And what better opportunity than this—an opportunity to meet over 300 women engineers who had been selected through nationwide merit tests? A whole new generation of potential women entrepreneurs! A whole mass of corporate executives are wealth and employment generators. I was very enthused!

As I reached the college, I saw the students all lined up to receive me despite the drizzle. They were all in their twenties, earnest, sincere, and a little bit unsure of themselves.

As I faced them in the auditorium, I asked them what they wanted to know from me. They said, "Everything!" Very smartly they had put the ball in my court. They were all bright and intelligent. What was it that I could talk about, which may not be a formal part of their degree course, but more or less left to themselves to learn by trial and error? Or even after some blunders.

I asked them if they wanted me to share with them the serious mistakes, if allowed to grow, which could become blunders in their lives. They responded with a collective yes. I was amazed how advice poured out of me, all based on the experiences of thirty five years of my service.

Here is what I suggested to them to be alert and careful about to avoid pitfalls and sufferings.

Focus on education completely right now and do not be in a hurry to settle down in marriage before your education is complete. There is an age for education, for right now you are protected, supported, and provided for. You can pay full attention to your studies. It will take much bigger effort to complete your education after marriage as a lot of other responsibilities will demand your time. Hence do not postpone completing your education. All other things can wait. Do not rush into marriage based on assurances because after marriage these assurances may remain unfulfilled for many reasons. So why make this the reason for a breach of promise in the future and hurt your marriage?

Try and be your own master by looking at options of self-employment, even if it means starting small. Make partnerships among yourselves. Being your own master and being in control of your own creativity is a big achievement. Try to be an employer rather than an employee. Explore these options before you look for jobs. Keep alive the fire within you to be your own master.

Be prepared for mobility. This is the age to be mobile, to explore the world, and not look for security and status quo. This is the time for growth, to be adventurous, and stay on top of the learning curve. It will not happen without you being willing to take newer challenges. Travelling will groom you to be tougher and dynamic. Do not resist change at this age.

Take on new learnings as they come your way. This means more and more training should be welcomed. Do not avoid it or postpone it. Even when married, do not let go any opportunity for training. Men do not wait, they go whenever they get a chance. Women tend to put family first all the time and sacrifice growth. And then they get left behind.

If there is an emergency at home which needs only you, then make the sacrifice, but not for any and every situation. Ensure and seek family support for your career growth.

Choose your partners in life most carefully, for this is going to change your life completely. Do not rush into a marriage. Have a long engagement and test out as much as is possible. A long engagement will reveal a lot about the person's qualities which may not be acceptable to you later on. Marriage is a risk; minimise the risk so that you make your life one of companionship and growth and not a relationship of sacrifice, life-long adjustments, and compromises.

Grow up as givers with no expectations from others. Give to your family, support those who need to be supported, but retain full control of your own resources. Do not pass over your financial controls to anyone else, lest you need permission even for spending from your own earnings. This is not being selfish but being in control and in command.

> *Give to your family, support those who need to be supported, retain full control of your own resources, do not pass over your financial controls to anyone else, lest you need permission even for spending from your own earnings.*

Pay for your comfort. Spend money for work you can delegate, to buy rest for yourself so that you can spend time on your own development and on activities you want to be involved in. Do not volunteer to do what you are not comfortable doing. Find ways and means to buy time for yourself.

Do not dress for others. Dress for your own selves. Dress as it makes you comfortable. Do not drink alcohol or smoke just to seek approval or get accepted. All consumption habits have to be a part of your authentic self.

All personal and professional decisions should be taken by you. Consult people you trust if you need to, but the decisions have to be your own, for you are going to live with them.

Find time for being with your own self, to listen to your inner voice. This is your own space. Live within your own self too. And let your space be your own, where you are just with your own self.

I told the girls that their education is to be lived-in-deeds by them. They were all a different category from those I usually met, as they were there because of their better use of education and now were aiming to be career women.

2
Be Yourself—Be Not a Man

This women's day I was in the company of a set of outstanding panellists comprising leading women professionals. They included chief executives of Britannia, Microsoft, IBM, JP Morgan, ICICI Bank, among others. Each one of them was a successful leader in her own right. The audience, too, was no less. The conference hall was packed with young professional women as well as self-employed ones, all qualified and enterprising. Each of us made our points without exaggerating or exceeding the given time. I came away from the event extremely enthused. It was evident that the Indian Woman had arrived.

Let me share what was put across that day.

Unwire the Hardwire: Be Aware

Research clearly shows that we are "hardwired" by the time we reach our twenties. Our attitudes and leadership qualities are already established. Our personal and professional orientations are already rooted and shaped by the time we start to work. The professional degree is more for honing professional skills and tools which may or may not alter our basic attitudes even if we are looking to change them. Hence we are complete packages by the time we arrive at the corporate doorstep.

Simply put, people do not change very much once they enter the work place. The changes that take place are mainly a matter of consolidation of strengths or a downward drift in behaviour that needs improvement.

The learning to be derived is: it is very important how we shape ourselves as girls. It will be easier if we groom ourselves the way we want to be when we are young, either way—as professionals or homemakers. Or both!

Give to others what you want for yourself

Today, with women coming into positions of power, they need to remain sensitive to others' needs. They must give to their own juniors and peers what they are looking for themselves. These include congratulating, mentoring, promotions, training, resources, support, understanding, appreciation, rewards, recognition, communication, sharing, and transparency. All that they want for themselves, they must equally become givers for those they supervise and lead, independent of whether they get what they need from their own seniors.

Women are perceived to be givers and sharers. Hence we must continue to build on this positive perception and belief. Perhaps we are "hardwired" on this when young. Hence we need not change what is our strength just because others do not endorse or support it.

Be the change you want to see

You want to see integrity, courage, discipline, hard work, fair play, welfare. Then you should provide them first. Do not just wish you had all this for yourself while you deny it to others. You should be the change and lead the way.

Develop skills of conflict resolution

Women today have a wide range of choices to make all the time. Earlier there were none whatsoever—exactly like the TV channels. From no TV, to one Doordarshan channel with only a black and white TV, to a wide variety of colour televisions with hundreds of competing channels. What a world of a difference!

Similarly, the world of a woman used to be her home and family. Her basic security was the gold ornaments she received at the time of marriage and from her husband and sons. Her journey was from her parents' home to her husband's. She was expected to serve unquestioningly. She personally owned nothing. Everything belonged to the elders and the husband. Anything asked from her, she was expected to part with. There was not much conflict, for there was no choice.

Today it is choices all the way, each choice filled with potential conflicts — professional demands and expectations, home responsibilities, children's needs, family relationships, time constraints, physical capabilities, financial status, social expectations, job insecurities, and many more. How do we handle these competing demands, full of contradictions and conflicts? How do we learn to deal with conflict management? Who teaches us? What kinds of solutions do we move towards? How much time do we take to learn? And do we?

> *Do not try and do it all yourself. Don't try to be perfect in all. Never hesitate to take help. Always give and share credit with all those who made it possible for you to succeed.*

One panellist said, "Each woman is a leader for she multitasks all the time. Women are not at the top of many organisations yet as they were late starters. Work-life balance is now a global issue. Women must learn to use and benefit from technology such as net meetings, video or teleconferences, etc."

Another panellist said, "Do not try and do it all yourself. Don't try to be perfect in all. Never hesitate to take help. Always give and share credit with all those who made it possible for you to succeed. Work or business is all about people. Be ready for change. Handle the challenge of change."

Accept that there are differences. Be yourself — be not a man.

3
Blurred, yet Moved

I am reminded of the time my father gave his old camera to my sister as a gift on her birthday. This camera could take only one negative at a time. Eager to use it right away, she got all of us properly lined up for her first shot. She insisted we say "cheese" as if it was not just a camera but a sound recorder as well. She took her time to click. But when the picture came out, she howled.

It was blurred! "Everybody moved," she cried.

In the world of women today, everything has moved. Life is not what it used to be. It has changed, and changed dramatically, for better and for worse.

One place where it has changed for the worse is Afghanistan. There is an unforgettable image which I saw on television—a group of women in blue burqas being whipped on their legs and backs by men. Their crime—they were seen on the street without a male escort, or *chowdhari* as they call them. In another reported case, a young woman's thumb was chopped off because she wore nail polish.

All this brought in many changes. Women were no longer seen in public. Women in Afghanistan, who had earlier worked while their men were engaged in battle, were banned from working outside their houses. Education became the preserve of men. Today, in 2002, barely 15 percent of the women in Afghanistan can read or write. Their access to health care is restricted as there are no lady doctors and they are not allowed to go to male doctors. An Afghan nurse, whose interview I saw on TV, said she had been a nurse in Kabul and had to flee the town. To survive, she had to beg on the streets. She said, "What could I do, I had to feed my children."

Today, in the name of religion and its totally distorted interpretation, the Taliban has enslaved women. In fact, women in Tihar prison in New Delhi may have more freedom than the women in Afghanistan.

> *For women in India, life has moved, even though it continues to be blurred for many.*

So, I come back to the camera and the picture my sister took. On the one hand, the Afghan women have descended into smoky dens, while there are innumerable others elsewhere in the world who are climbing to the very top. They are being educated and trained to go wherever they want. They are setting their goals and creating the road-maps to achieve them. They are being supported in their activities, or even doing them on their own. There is no field where they are not making their presence felt, be it the defence forces, civil governance, corporate management, scientific or medical research, education, creativity, or physical endurance. For them it's a matter of utilising the available opportunities to the maximum.

On the domestic front too, the picture has changed for many, although not to that extent. Women want a greater say in the choice of their life partners. No longer are there *pandals* of dowry display during weddings. The family size is small, for women choose to space and time their motherhood to balance their professional duties with parenting. For this section of women, times have changed, or they themselves have changed the situations around them. They have removed the blur and let it be known what is acceptable and what is not. But these are the courageous and fortunate few.

For a large cross-section of women in India, life is still blurred. A woman is still not sure of what use her education is. Does she have the right to continue her education as much as she wants? Who will she marry, why, and when? Will her husband and his parents allow her to work outside the home?

Will she have control over her own earnings? Will she be allowed to take care of her parents, brothers, and sisters in case of need? Will she be able to retain her identity or will she lose it completely, change her name, and have to start all over again? Will she have any rights on her husband's earnings? Will she be able to decide when she would like to become a mother, and how many times? Can she live away from her husband's home if her job so demands? Can she organise domestic help to allow her to get some rest when she returns home after a long day's work? Can she return to her parents' home in case of need, or is that no longer her home?

For women in India, life has moved, even though it continues to be blurred for many. And these questions are a consequence and testimony of that movement.

4
Dawn of a New Generation

I was invited to speak at the National Integration Camp of NCC girl cadets. This event came on the heels of a number of incidents of rapes, assaults, and molestation of girls in Delhi, Mumbai, and elsewhere. Against this background, and with anguish in my heart, this is what I told these young girls.

"You girls are already different. Remember this always for the rest of your life. The very fact that you are wearing slacks or, for those in sports, tracksuits, which have traditionally been male dresses, shows you are imbibing all the sound traits which are attributed to sensible men, like bravery, endurance, courage, responsibility, giving protection, and economic independence.

"And you girls are becoming one *plus* one, that is, learning the best qualities of sensible men along with your own qualities of sensible women, which are patience, compassion, forbearance, giving, sharing, communication, care and concern, sensitivity, appreciation, recognition, and so on. Hence, you are doubly equipped now.

"You are learning to be strong and sensitive. Therefore, you will be different from the rest in the sense you will be stronger, more secure, and yet remain sensitive to others' needs. So, please do not ever forget your acquired learning.

"Already your way of thinking, talking, walking, and responding is going through a change without you realising it, and it will continue to evolve. Others will notice the change, while to you it may not be evident.

"You girls are also going to be different, for you will not be easily subjugated, unless you, yourself, give in and surrender. You are learning teamwork, discipline, organisational skills and self-management. Do not let these learnings lie dormant or get lost. Go and lead from the front wherever you are.

"Those of you who belong to the villages, go and be the *panch* and the *sarpanch*, while following your vocations. In *panchayats*, 33 percent of the seats are reserved for you. It does not matter which political party you align with, as long as you carry your values, training, ethics, and morality into it. If that party does not recognise your values, stand and fight as an independent. But do not compromise on your values. The nation needs grass-roots, values-based leadership.

"If you are in towns, go and fight the municipal elections, become student-leaders in your colleges and universities, and provide the moral face with a moral base. Pick up the right issues with social responsibility. Practise your NCC values of discipline and patriotism. This is what all this training is all about.

"The nation is investing in a select few of you, when actually this training is required to be given to every young man and woman of this country. I cannot imagine patriotism developing in the youth of this country without NCC training in schools, colleges, and universities.

"Therefore, my girls, you have three choices after your NCC training—join the armed forces, the police services, or become political leaders. These ought to be your priorities after what you are learning today. You may marry and become good mothers. This is your personal choice. But for joining the armed forces or police services or taking on political or public responsibility, you have no choice. You have got to shoulder these responsibilities. If you will not, then who else will?"

When I said all this to those NCC cadets, in no way did I intend to undermine any other vocation or job. I was provoking them to be ready for the most challenging ones, basically to drive home the point that they must prepare themselves for the toughest situations. Whatever else comes after these responsibilities will be easy for them in view of their training and additional learning.

I was also provoking them to use their training to remain different and show the difference in their personal lives too. I challenged them to announce to their parents that they dare not give dowries for them in their marriage. And not let the men they propose to settle down with hold them back from realising their full potential or forcibly inhibiting or circumscribing their mobility.

> *Our country, our India, needs each one of these bright, enthusiastic, motivated, hard working, trained, patriotic girls.*

I tried to put the onus on these girls for taking greater responsibility, and to help them get out of any feeling of lethargy or dependence on others. I told them that they had to be equal providers, hereafter, in all respects—as much as their sensible brothers—for their parents and their families.

I asked Major General P. K. Singh, AVSM, who was present there whether the girls were being taught self-defence. When he said no, I requested, "Sir, do not let them go without learning it. These girls have to be trained to protect themselves and others, and when not in uniform they ought to have full confidence to strike back at the prowlers."

I asked the organisers to seek a budget for this training or else let the girls contribute towards the cost of a teacher. Or perhaps, an NGO or industry group could come forward to sponsor a teacher.

If the girls of NCC too are going to be victims of prowling men, and are not going to be capable of giving a black eye to the eve-teasers when the situation demands, then who will? Let the prisons be the place for men with black eyes, identifiable from a distance with a mark left on their faces for all times.

Our country, our India, needs each one of these bright, enthusiastic, motivated, hard working, trained, patriotic girls, in shirts and slacks as against the backless and almost topless *cholis* at cocktails parties, to lead and show the way with ethics, decency, and morality — to be the real soldiers.

"You will be the dawn of a new generation," was my parting salute to these young Indian girl cadets.

5
Double Standards

I was invited to inaugurate and speak at a workshop on "Breaking Gender Stereotypes", jointly organised by Zakir Hussain College and Women's Development Centre, University of Delhi. It was a workshop to examine the practices which were reinforcing our social attitudes and responses towards gender issues, and the practices we needed to change. Many eminent social scientists, academicians, authors, counsellors, research scholars, and students of the subject were present.

In my inaugural speech, I highlighted some practices which are seen to be reinforcing gender stereotypes and from which we need to break away if we really want to bring about social development and all-round progress.

The first one is the nature of advertisements on television. Since TV is a powerful medium and reaches all homes daily and repeatedly, we need to see how the advertisers are projecting gender issues. I gave the example of two prominent advertisements of Life Insurance of India (LIC) and Unit Trust of India (UTI), being aired daily on television. These were clearly examples of gender stereotypes. Both give the impression that household savings are meant for the education of the son and the marriage of the daughter. In other words, repeatedly giving the message that education is a priority for sons while marriage is the priority for daughters, and reinforcing the idea that sons are an investment and daughters are an expenditure. Also, as if the marriages of sons need no expenses and only daughters' marriages do.

This, no doubt, is a social reality. But why should it continue to be reinforced? Does it not need a change? And how is this to be done? If we want to change such attitudes, the advertisement ought to say that income from LIC or UTI is a big support to educate our children and then prepare them for their careers. And the marriage of either a son or a daughter could be one of the reasons of expenditure, not the only one.

Other areas in which gender stereotypes are habitually reinforced are college festivals and so-called religious practices. In most of the college festivals, one of the most popular events is the fashion show — girls walking the ramp with the audience, consisting mainly of boys, cheering and whistling. I really do not know whether having fashion shows as a part of college festivals is necessary. I would prefer to see girls participating in more varied and creative activities, such as group singing, debates, plays, and quiz programmes, with equal fervour. In other words, the focus could be more on all-round creativity rather than on what the girls look like or how they walk.

Another concern are the religious practises. In many of our Hindu festivals, it is the woman who fasts for her husband and prays for his good health and longevity. There is not a single occasion when the man does so for his wife. Why should there not be a *Karva Chauth* for both, the wife for her husband and the husband for his wife? Will this not increase her social status and make her feel more respected?

And why are we continuing the purdah system, or the burqas? Don't women have the right to see the sun directly? Who is perpetuating this? We all are. The society of men and women — and the women reconciling and compromising with these gender stereotypes all the time. No visibly collective challenge has emerged to these practises. No students union has taken it up, nor any religious group either.

And let me bring up the issue of *sindoor*, the *mangalsutra* and the red bangles, which are the visible indicators that the woman is married. But what about the Indian men? Why doesn't the culture provide some visible indicators of marital status for men? Can you imagine men accepting any such thing? Why is everything to be done by women? And women, too, accept and practice these stereotypes without much resistance!

A society, to change, and change fast, has to demonstrate a collective urge to change. Since this has not happened, we are continuing to reinforce gender stereotypes and holding back our daughters from realising their full potential. We forget that when we educate our daughters and they move to another house, we give the other families educated daughters-in-law, and when our sons marry, we receive educated daughters-in-law.

> *Collectively, society will become what individuals think and do. Double standards only create a society of hypocrites.*

When will we understand that we must first give to society what we want for ourselves? And it is in doing so that we will question and change the wrong practices and traditions. Collectively, society will become what individuals think and do. Double standards only create a society of hypocrites. And that is what we are becoming today. Who do we blame it on?

6
Early Marriage: Till the Tears Run Dry

In my review of our rural project located on the outskirts of Delhi, I wanted to take feedback from the girls who were undergoing a vocational training course. They were all in the age group of 15 to 18 years. I was extremely curious to know and understand what kind of change, if any, was taking place around them and in their minds. In the current environment and media exposure, so many social issues and social evils concerning girls and daughters are being highlighted. I wanted to understand the impact on them.

Interestingly, also present in another course being conducted in the same premises, were women *sarpanch* and *panch* of nearby villages. They had come for the *panchayat* training programme being conducted by Chandni Bedi Taneja, Project Head, Rural, for these women.

Hence there was a mix of two generations—the young and the old. But let me tell you about the older group first.

The senior women were completely illiterate. They had never been to school. They were elected through the 33 percent quota reserved for women in *panchayats*. They were expected to represent their respective villages on all issues concerning them—issues which impacted their day-to-day lives.

And it was evident how ill-equipped they were. Not because they did not know their problems, but because they were ignorant about what they could do. They felt helpless in all respects, and had resigned themselves to their fate and circumstances, till this training, which was making them aware of their capacity and capability to help themselves.

They did not know which person was responsible for what. Who were their officials? What were the government schemes? What were their resources? And who would listen to them? They had issues of water, school, teachers, illiteracy of their daughters-in-law, disputes over water, drains—all to do with their daily lives. We could not know what the men in their villages had to say, but I am sure their needs and priorities would have been different.

> *If they have enough time for parties, festivals, and all other forms of entertainment, why not also for national service which builds their country?*

We switch over to the girls now. All of them were school dropouts, some after class five, some after class seven and some even after class nine. I asked them the reasons for not continuing with their studies. They said it was because there were no girls' schools within walking distance of their homes. Their parents, particularly their fathers, did not agree to send them to far away schools, all the more if it was a co-educational one. Also, the fathers did not give money for anything to do with their education.

I asked them what they wanted. Each one of them said they wanted to continue their schooling. But there were no schools close by. There was no transport available to take them to schools which were some distance away, even if the girls were to collect and go together. Their fathers did not want them to study further, for they believed it was a waste of time since they were anyway going to be housekeepers or work alongside their husbands tilling the land.

They had another problem. When they drop out of school, they are told, "Now that you are out of school, you will be married off." And none of them wanted to get married just yet.

I asked them what goes on in their minds when, on the television, they see girls reaching for the skies. They said they too want to make their parents proud, but the parents did not understand that. No one listened to them.

"What do you do then?" I asked.

They said, they cry.

"Then what happens?" I quizzed further.

"Our mother comes and tells us this is the way it is with girls, so we had better accept it," they said.

Who blames whom? Why would mothers and such fathers in the villages bear and nourish girls? Are these girls not a burden of some sort?

Is just targeting the doctors who conduct female foeticide enough? While it is necessary to stop the doctors, but what else? Who all are working on these fathers—through the *panchayats* in particular and the village groups in general?

India's destiny lies in working with the *panchayats* and the village communities—if these girls have to be stopped from crying and their mothers to stop telling them that this is what is the destiny of women.

Our young students from senior schools and universities, boys and girls, need to work in the villages as an expression of the community's volunteer *shram* or *seva*. There is no other way to sensitise the urban youth to what is being taken for granted by them. If they have enough time for parties, festivals, and all other forms of entertainment, why not also for national service which builds their country?

I have no doubt that if this volunteer work becomes an integral part of our education system and national psyche, it will truly provide the much needed integration through community service. Then all forms of wastage, greed, selfish living, wasteful consumption, value for hard work, preventive health care, respect for natural resources will not be mere topics in text books learning seen and experienced as life skills.

Our youth has the time and energy. We only need to inspire and help plan their direction. Planners and administrators owe this to the country.

Or else these, and many other similarly placed girls, will keep crying till their tears run dry!

7
Girl Child Education: Duty or Liability?

On my previous visit to the rural project, Navjyoti, at Bhondsi, Gurgaon, Chandni Bedi Taneja, the Project Head, Rural, shared some interesting observations about the village girls who were attending the ongoing summer camp at the Navjyoti Centre. I asked her to let me know a typical girl's situation, in her own words, for sharing with a larger audience. The reality expressed in these words underscores the gigantic national challenges we have before us—in terms of attitudes needed to be changed and resources to be put in place.

Here is what she wrote. This reveals the reality of a place just twenty five kilometres from the capital of our country.

"I get up at 6:00 a.m., milk the buffaloes, perform household chores such as cleaning the house and utensils, fetching water, cooking for everyone at home and sending my younger brother to school. In the afternoon I take rest for two hours and then give fodder to the buffaloes in the evening, again clean the house, cook food, wash utensils and go to sleep," said Renu who had come to attend stitching classes.

For most of the girls in the age group of 12 to 16 years in rural areas, these are the customary tasks in their everyday lives. The only aspect missing from their routine is school. It was astounding to see that all the girls attending the camp, except one, were school dropouts. The one who was studying was in class ten, but was not sure whether she would be permitted to continue her studies after this. Yet another girl said that she was not allowed to continue her studies after seventh class by her elder brother, who himself was eighth pass-out and could not accept that his sister could be more educated than him. The centre was flooded with such stories, which only highlight the inequalities in our society that are deep-rooted and reflect gender bias.

> *A movement should be launched with the aim of eliminating gender discrimination and gender disparity in education systems.*

Despite the efforts made by the government on a rights-based approach and increase in the overall enrolment rate, education of the girl child still remains a distant dream. Moreover, increase in enrolment does not necessarily indicate the number of children going to schools, as there are challenges of regular attendance and retention rate. Statistics reveal that 83.2 percent boys and 75.1 percent girls attended school in the age group of 6 to 10 years, while in the age group of 15 to 17 years, 54.8 percent boys and 32.8 percent girls in rural India attended schools. Time is ticking away to achieve the Millennium Development Goals which aim to promote quality education to "all children". However, gender parity and gender equality remain issues of concern.

Much can be attributed to the supply demand paradigm. Given the scarcity of middle and secondary schools for girls, many of them drop out after completing primary education. Parents do not want to send their girls to co-ed schools. "Girls' secondary school is at a distance of 6 to 8 kilometres from our village. We are not allowed to walk down alone," said Babita, a class seven dropout. "So we used to go in groups. Since my friends discontinued studies, I was left with no other option but to stay at home."

While other issues continue to persist, social and cultural factors deny girls equal opportunities, compared to boys. Having accepted their fates for having daughters born to them, parents are reluctant to send their daughters to school as they believe that the education will be of no use—their girls do not have to take up jobs after marriage.

The beliefs pass down from one generation to the next and female illiteracy continues.

Another factor attributed is the lack of interest of the girls themselves in studies. However, the underlying causes of their lack of interest are the inefficacy of school management systems, lack of teachers, and quality of education. Other causes of attrition include child marriage and lack of toilet facilities — a need at the menstruating age. While the boys are sent to private schools, girls are denied the facilities available in private schools. Most of the times, girls lack the confidence to return to mainstream education due to an increased gap in studies.

Economic constraints also prevent parents from sending their girls to school as they perceive the girl's education as a liability. They cannot afford to spend both on her dowry as well as her studies. There are also hidden obstacles that hinder her educational attainment as she spends time doing household chores and taking care of her siblings and little or no time is left for studies.

Our experience of the summer camp tells us that there are a host of factors leading to inequity in education of the girl child. A number of such cases go unnoticed as the common perception is that enough is being done on gender issues.

There is a need to address these problems holistically. Extensive surveys are required to find out the exact number of cases of school dropouts among girls so that work on the root cause of the problem can be done. Counselling to parents and girls, preventing child marriage, developing infrastructure and facilities in government schools, and greater involvement of community and *panchayat* needs to be included in the projects.

A movement should be launched with the aim of eliminating gender discrimination and gender disparity in education systems through concrete actions at global, national, state, district, and community levels. This requires effective and consistent partnerships between the government, NGOs, corporates, panchayats, schools, teachers, parents, and communities.

The questions we need to answer are: Who initiates coordination and forges partnerships? Who trains whom for initiatives? Who is best placed to do so? Whose duty is it? Is anyone accountable for this at all? Should this not be an issue for measures for promotions of government officials, grants to various bodies and re-elections of politicians?

Perhaps, not yet.

8
How Can We Be Heard?

Last fortnight I was at the National Conference of Women Professionals. The audience comprised women in governance roles and management. Most of them were in the middle-level leadership positions. I was invited for an interactive session with them.

The first question was: "How can we (women) be heard?"

My answer was direct and straight. "You will be heard for your competence," I said. "You will be heard not because of the decibels you produce, but because of your reputation for professional capability. Others will want to hear you more when you are silent. Often, your silence will speak louder than words. Your colleagues will probe you. They will even provoke you to read your mind. You are of value!

"Remember to speak only if you have something useful to say. Being a learner and a good listener is equally respected and noticed. Do not speak for the sake of speaking or to mark your presence. Speak only to add value.

"Remember never to raise the pitch of your voice. Speak softly, with measured words. Hear your own self while speaking. Never ever be critical of the previous speakers or of the views they expressed. Thank them for their perspectives and then offer your own. If you are known for your competence, people will wait to hear your views. In fact, they might even ask you to say something if you have remained silent for any reason. If you are known only to speak for the sake of speaking, then people will wait for you to shut up and even interrupt while you are speaking. The bottom line is that you will be heard only due to your competence and capability. If you have it, then your contribution will always be looked forward to and valued. To be heard raise your worth, not your voice."

The second question was: "How do we raise our worth?"

My answer was, "By respecting your own work, and regular and daily preparation.

> *The bottom line is that you will be heard only due to your competence and capability.*

Do not put your work on hold at every home or personal pressure, as some women do. Work has to be kept on a parallel priority, to run alongside all other priorities. And it must have its time and space. Women, as mothers, wives, daughters-in-law, or relatives, often tend to give lower priority to work than all other needs, even when there is no urgency. This makes others take women for granted.

"Please volunteer for advanced training opportunities. Keep yourselves up to date on the latest at work. Do not postpone learning. It must run parallel if you wish to remain on centre stage."

The third question was: "What do we do if we are sidelined?"

My answer was, "Make sidelines the centre of your commitment and excel in it. Whatever you get, make that work the centre of your attention. Give it your best. Find ways and reasons to like it. Make it grow as much as you can. Think and be creative in it. Do not sulk. Take it or leave it. Exercise that choice. If you do not leave, because you do not have any other choice, or you want to stay despite the situation, then adopt it. Mother it! Do not orphan it. Nurture it. Reward it. By your ignoring and sulking, you punish yourself and your work. Never punish your work, for it hurts your juniors even more. They look up to you for leadership, guidance, care, growth, and recognition—all that you want from your own seniors.

"Learn the art of self-reward. Dependence on external recognition creates dependence. Train to be independent. Or else it will be a weakness others could exploit. Then recognition will become favours done in the expectation of returns of all kinds, which may compromise you professionally or personally. Let rewards happen naturally. Let others wonder what is so special in your work that keeps you contented and happy. Remember, no one has time for complaining individuals. State your mind when there is an opportunity to do so. You are the best judge. Meanwhile, learn to be centred around yourself."

I then asked if I could also ask a question of the women in the audience. I queried, "Where is your next generation?" They answered, "Very few are interested in networking."

The audience mostly comprised middle-aged women and very few were in their thirties. "Remember," I said, "We need to co-opt and prepare the younger generation to pass on baton. Also, to deepen the expectation of making a difference. We need to build on the positive image which people still have of women in leadership and decision-making positions—we have exceptions of course!"

In the end, I wondered if these issues did not equally apply to men also. Yes, indeed they do, but certainly more for women in management roles. The primary reason is that women in professional leadership positions are the first generation leaders. The culture they work in is not their creation. It is inherited.

Change is taking its time and also its toll. Women must not pass on the hurt, to ensure that these instances of being sidelined or "not being heard" are decreased!

9
It's Good to be a Saheli

I was at an annual function of Saheli, an organisation in Boston founded by some very well-established professional women and a few men. The volunteers of Saheli offer support and friendship to South Asian immigrant women and their families in many capacities, mainly in the areas of family discord, domestic crisis, and legal and immigration issues.

I went to the function as I had great respect for the cause and fully supported the work they did. And I appreciated how vital it was to continue doing so. Without Saheli and other similar organisations, many women would not have known where to go when abused or beaten, and when they could take it no more.

We, as Indians, know how alluring these overseas marriage proposals are to the parents of daughters. Since many decades, and this is something that continues even now, getting a daughter married to an Indian overseas who was stated to be "well-settled" was a fascinating prospect and remained a dream for many an Indian parent. This despite the many sad stories that were reported and the well-publicised accounts of how brutally these women were treated and sent home packing, or abandoned, with no place to go.

Many of these women needed a *saheli* or friend, and an organisation like Saheli. *The Asian Family Violence Report* (Boston, November 2000), in a study of the Chinese, Cambodian, Korean, South Asian, and Vietnamese communities in Massachusetts, revealed some dominant beliefs among the South Asian families caught in the cycle of family violence. Here are some of the highlights as presented by the focus group members about the prevailing mindset as to why many battered women continue to live in abusive relationships.

- A married woman is believed to become the property of her husband after marriage and is seen as no longer belonging to her parents.
- She cannot turn to her own family for help once she is married and her parents are not supposed to intervene.
- The in-laws play a critical role in "family violence", especially in dowry disputes.
- Women who leave their husband's home, even if it is an abusive one, will experience a tremendous stigma.
- The influence of factors such as financial insecurity, visa status (where applicable), dependence on their husbands, and uncertainty about life after divorce were also some of the major issues.

So where do we go from here? Let me share with you what was suggested that Saheli should consider doing beyond what they were already doing. Basically, this was a three-step strategy.

First, prepare a prevention and awareness package. This means rewinding and going to the source, that is, the parents. And airing of subtle messages through our television channels (in India) that all that glitters overseas may not be gold. Hence, they should always verify all details properly before they hand over their daughters to strangers.

Additionally, they could put together an information brochure or a toolkit about support systems in case of need, which could be picked up at visa counters. And then, they could broadcast soft messages offering accessible support on the US-based Indian and Asian TV and radio channels.

The Asian Family Violence Report clearly revealed that out of every 100 men who beat their wives, 67 were frustrated and angry. Why not devise plans and create opportunities to encourage and promote *Art of Living* or anger management courses as part of the counselling and other support services?

Second, the *Response plan*, which Saheli has already put in place. It can find greater support through more volunteers in the fields of legal services, training, fund raising, counselling, and law enforcement. Why not support short spots on and by the local Indian channels as public interest messages?

Third, the *Partnership plan*. Network with other NGOs working in the same social service field. Share research studies. Form groups of "helped" women who are now able to assist those who need help. Work out the economics of prevention of family violence and do advocacy work with donors and agencies for additional support, while explaining that this prevents agony and avoids huge waste of money from the state exchequer.

And finally, not to rely only on the internet but instead also to reach out, through as many different means of communication as possible, to women in need, from Asia in general and India in particular. In most cases, these women are not yet internet savvy.

Despite all this, I have no doubt that Saheli will continue to be needed by many parents who will continue to fall into the trap of false glitter.

> *All that glitters overseas may not be gold. Hence they should always verify all details properly before they hand over their daughters to strangers.*

10
Know This Law and Prevent Violence

It is interesting to see how nature, at times, conspires. As I wrote the title and started writing this article, a young woman, Rashmi, came to see me. She presented me her about-to-be released book, *Woman of the Elements*. Rashmi and I had met earlier, too, on other occasions.

But this meeting was different. I asked her the thought behind her book. She said, "Sufferings from domestic violence." I was taken aback. This was exactly what I was planning to write about, so that people understood the essence of the new law on domestic violence and did not rely on hearsay.

Let me tell you what Rashmi told me. I have her permission to narrate the story.

"Mrs Bedi, I woke up this morning, switched on some music, drank a cup of tea, read the paper, tickled my son to wake him up, and hugged my daughter awake. It was a beautiful morning, my everyday morning.

"But it wasn't so for 10 years of my lifewhen I would wake up in a cold sweat everyday, wondering what anger, what abuse, what violence I would have to face that day. I wore full-sleeves tops and Chinese collars for 10 years to hide the bruises I carried on my body.

"Mine was an arranged marriage. I had been working as an advertising professional for two or three years prior to that. But violence against women cuts across the boundaries of class and social strata. Our biggest drawback as women is that when abuse takes place against us, we do not speak up about it. We hide behind 'acceptability', 'decency'. We shrivel up in silence.

"I did not even tell my family, not for five years. My daughter was four when I first went back to my parents with a broken rib and a smashed face.

> *Under the new law, all these acts of domestic violence are specific offences.*

Not the first instance of violence—it was a common occurrence for me. But that was the first time that I sensed a need in myself to get out of the vile situation. But my husband came to my family and wept, begged, pleaded. And I went back. And I had a second child. My husband gloated, 'Now you can never leave.' And the violence escalated.

"I had a mother-in-law in the house, but she added to the problems. According to her, *'Ma-baap toh pait kaat kar apnee betiyon ko dete hain,'* (parents sacrifice everything to give gifts to their daughters), *'Biwiyon ko to property aur paison ke baarey mein kuch batana nahin chahiye,'* (wives should not be told anything about property and finances), and so on. Strange words coming from a woman who completely controlled the purse-strings of the family! And when confronted with the violence meted out to me, she would respond with, *'Toh kya hua? Jo tumhari kismet,'* (So what, it is your fate).

"I had been given a vacant floor in this large house in a posh south Delhi colony, with the not-so-posh words, *'Hamaari families mein to ladki waalon se sab kuch aata hai,'* (in our families everything comes from the girl's family). So I worked harder, took up short projects and assignments and tried to build a home, along with its furniture and everything else that came with it. From the curtains to the carpets, everything came from my earnings. My husband did not pay for even a glass.

"As time went by and his violence and womanising got worse, it started telling on the children. My daughter, a brilliant little girl, became quiet and withdrawn. My son went into a shell completely. He would not talk—he would withdraw into his own world when confronted with loud voices. He was put into the special needs section at the school that he was attending, not because he had any learning disability, but because of his emotional problems.

"I did not want to stay alive any more. I had died enough every day. Then I used to look at my children and wonder, if I die, what will happen to them? I knew then that I would fight for my life and that of my children. I somehow picked up courage and decided to leave, with both my kids, and go to my grandmother's house. I finally earned my freedom after a very long, bitter, and expensive struggle for divorce.

"Today I am a woman of all elements—air, water, fire, and earth—who picked herself up from ashes to rebuild her life, along with those of her children."

The new Domestic Violence Act was notified a few days ago. What if it had been there earlier? And Rashmi knew of it and took the courage to use it? Then the husband and the mother-in-law would have been forced to mend their ways or face imprisonment for a whole year.

Let me explain how. Under the new law, all the acts of domestic violence are specific offences, namely, physical or mental abuse for any reason, addiction, extramarital relationships, unlawful demands, harassment, threat, insult, ridicule, name calling, deprivation of economic or financial resources, alienation of assets, and so on.

Anyone can complain on behalf of the aggrieved woman. The Magistrate can call the members of the household and hear what they have to say. He can counsel, direct, or punish as the case may be. It is a civil, summary proceeding. Violation of orders can call for imprisonment of one year, or fine, or both.

There is an essential provision for appointment of protection officers and NGOs as service providers. Homes could be visited by them for reporting or follow-ups.

Rashmi could have got protection had this law come in force earlier. Her children would not have suffered as much as they did. She could have continued to stay in her own home if she wanted to. Her mother-in-law, too, would have come under home visits of the protection officer. All this is the new law.

This law is for women who need help. At no stage should it be misused by them. Magistrates and protection officers are there to provide justice and are not pro-women or anti-men. They are there to prevent distress in genuine cases.

11
Let's Help Ourselves

I was in Goa for the Women's Day celebrations organised by the Goa Women's Commission. What I saw there angered me and I am sure those of you who read this will feel the same way.

Since I had some time to spare between two meetings, I requested my hosts to drive me around the town so that I could get a feel of the city. They asked me if I would like to visit the red-light area. This was in Vasco da Gama. I said yes, and we went there. This was not the first time that I was visiting a red-light area where commercial sex goes on. I saw young girls and women thronging the road and by-lanes, dressed in provocative clothes, and wearing heavy make-up. There were a lot of men hovering around, and some were bargaining with the women.

What angered me most was the presence of a large number of pubs and liquor vends in the area. I was told that the men first come and drink here and even force the girls to sit and drink with them. So the commercial sex activity is between two drunk individuals. I feel that while these pubs and liquor shops earn a small revenue for the government, it is at a huge social cost. In this case, the men, after drinking alcohol, behave like beasts and exploit the women for their sexual needs. The latter do not complain, for they are in the business of selling their bodies. I asked my friend from the Goa State Women's Commission whether the women in the Commission were doing anything about it. She said no one listens to them. I felt extremely sad and angry.

It was with this anger within me that I returned for my appointment where I was to address a public meeting of women.

When I reached the venue, I was informed by the Chairman of the Goa Women's Commission that none of the invitees, that is, the Deputy Chief Minister and the local MLA, who had committed to attend, had arrived, and that there was no message from them either. Even this basic courtesy was lacking from them. Since the meeting was in a public maidan, there was already a large gathering of women seated with the men standing on the flanks.

> *Women in India must rise above party or caste lines and get organised to raise their voice against social evils because it is the women who suffer the most.*

When I addressed the assembly of women and men, I told them that women will never be heard as long as they continue to vote for politicians who break their promises. Women in India must rise above party or caste lines and get organised to raise their voice against social evils because it is the women who suffer the most when there is a prevalence of alcoholism, pubs, gambling, casinos, and prostitution. They must let the local politicians know that they will reject them outright if they do not ensure removal of these social evils.

I learnt that despite women's protests, the Goa Government had allowed the opening of casinos in the state. Hence, Goa became the first Indian state to have a casino. On asking the women there what the government had to say to their protests, I was told that they blamed the previous government for having made the policy and, further, that these same politicians, before coming into power, had been against the casinos.

Besides just holding Women's Day Celebrations, we need to understand that ensuring the rights of women is the duty of the society. A healthy and educated woman is a national asset. She contributes to the prosperity of the society just as an illiterate, poor, and unhealthy woman contributes to the increase in its liabilities through the production of weak, malnourished, and neglected children. Hence, issues concerning women are not for women alone to solve. They concern the whole society and the nation. The earlier we collectively recognise this, the faster will we move towards becoming a stronger nation.

For this, we do not have to wait for the politicians. We can start from our own homes, neighbourhoods, *bastis*, villages, and schools.

12
Marriage and Identity Crisis

The recent outburst of a Bollywood star, raring to join politics, categorically pronouncing that women after marriage ought to give up their maiden name, made me ask myself, "What is the issue in keeping the maiden name and what is it that needs to be appreciated before such pronouncements are made?"

We know that the name is the identity of a person. Some get their given name by default while others get it after considerable thought, fanfare, religious rituals, and social ceremonies. These children are "welcomed" and loved and are often given a name which carries the vision or dream of their elders and parents. In many given names there is a family linkage, a value vision, or a spiritual dimension.

All people, therefore, have a name which gives them an identity. And as we grow up, we build our reputations around it. We create our network of associates and friends. Some create a special place for themselves in the society by their exceptional achievements and become known far and wide. The right to this image is not the monopoly of any single gender, it belongs to anyone who strives and achieves success.

Then why have women in India been made to change their identity on marriage from times immemorial? On marriage the pandits give a totally new name to the incoming daughters-in-law. Not only is the surname replaced, sometimes she even gets a new first name.

This means a whole new start for her, all over again. All that was achieved, created, and built goes entirely into the archives and can get carried forward under a new name and identity only. Such a woman, when faced with the older times, keeps answering the question, "Are you not the same person?"

This happened to me. I was often asked, and still am, "Are you not the same Kiran Peshawaria who used to play tennis? Or studied at Sacred Heart School? Or at the Punjab University, Chandigarh? Or came for a declamation contest to my college?" This is just the tip. The iceberg melts away. That first hard-earned identity or lovingly nurtured name now rests in the inner recesses of one's own self. Does a man ever face such a situation? How would he feel? Particularly when it is something imposed and one is given no choice?

So when one says that women ought to drop their earlier name or surname on marriage and take the identity of their husband, one must keep in mind many sensitivities and perspectives, including the changing times. Today, more and more women are marrying when they have established and earned identities of their own. They would not like to lose them after marriage. They now also want to preserve their father's family names as daughters, both for identity as well as for family bonding. Many are, in fact, adding on and not subtracting from their earlier surnames. They are hyphenating the married name with their maiden name. This is the choice they are exercising.

So who is to decide? The woman, of course, who is the loser or gainer in the process. And this right ought to be respected, just as it is the case for men. They are never expected to take up the surnames of their wives. It's just not the issue for them, while they too have a choice! But when has one ever heard of this? Besides, Indian pandits have never found anything wrong with names of sons-in-laws to want to change them!

Interestingly, I was at a round-table meet of visiting experts from Netherlands a few days ago. And since this "name" issue was fresh in my mind, I asked those who were at my table, how it was in Netherlands. Were women keeping their maiden names?

I did not have to go far to get the answer. The person sitting next to me was none other than the Mayor of the City of Almere, Annemarie Jorritsma-Lebbink. She said that women in her country have the legal right to give their children their own surname by virtue of a legislated Civil Law, Book 1—Title 2: Right for the name. Here are the relevant sections 4, 5, and 8, of the Dutch law as given to me by the Mayor.

> *Women around the world are now choosing to preserve and protect their hard-earned identities.*

"If a child is born in a legal relationship, both parents declare in front of a civil servant on the occasion of the registration of the birth or earlier (before birth) which of their both surnames it will have."

Section 8 further says, "Next children in the same relationship will have the same name."

It was only in default of registration that the child gets the name of the father.

Women around the world are now choosing to preserve and protect their hard-earned identities. The new breed of politicians need to wake up to the current realities.

Or they will be relegated to history in times ahead!

13
Not Born Free

At times, when I come across situations of the kind I am going to narrate, I feel that being born a girl in my country is really a curse for many girls and their parents.

I was in Madhya Pradesh for an event to promote my book when I received a request for help from a family living in the city. They told me, over the phone, that their daughter, a computer software engineer, was married and living in a neighbouring city. She had not been allowed to meet her parents or even receive their telephone calls, by her husband and in-laws. Every time the parents telephoned her, the in-laws did not pass on the message to her. They either said that she was not at home or that she could not take the call. They rudely put the phone down. The family told me that they were very worried as they had no news of the well-being of their daughter. They were helpless and did not know anyone who could guide and help them how to get in touch with their daughter.

I took down their daughter's name and telephone number and assured them that I would, myself, convey their message to their daughter and request her to contact them. I felt touched by their faith in me and called their daughter from my mobile phone.

When someone picked up the call, I gave my name and said I had a message for the girl. I mentioned her name. The gentleman who had answered passed on the phone to someone else. I repeated that I was speaking from another city and that I had an urgent message for their daughter-in-law. When prompted for the message, I asked if she could contact her parents soon as they were very worried about her. When I asked who was taking the message, the person said that he was the father-in-law. Now I could guess that the phone had initially been received by the girl's husband, who had passed it on to his father. My phone call was abruptly disconnected by the father-in-law. I could sense that the fears of the girl's parents were not unfounded and all did not appear to be well.

> *When I see situations of the kind I am going to narrate, I feel that being born a girl in my country is really a curse for many girls and their parents.*

On my return to Delhi, I called up the girl's home again. Again, it appeared that it was the husband who answered the phone. He feigned to be an outsider who did not even want to take a message and abruptly put the phone down. I called up again and said that basic courtesy demanded that even a stranger in the house should not disconnect the phone and should at least take a message. He then reluctantly wrote down my phone number, saying that the girl was not at home.

An hour later, I got a call from the father-in-law, who asked me what the message was. I told him that it was for his daughter-in-law. He said that I should give the message to him. I asked him why the daughter-in-law could not take the message. He said he would not allow her to. He also asked me the capacity in which I was calling. I said it was as a concerned government servant, doing her duty. He again banged the phone down.

I then called up the area police station and passed on the information to them. Later, I was informed that the girl's parents had been called by the in-laws, threatened, and asked to withdraw their complaint, or they would have to suffer. This scared them and they decided to take a train that night and go to their daughter's house immediately. They called me on the phone before leaving. I advised them to go to the police station, take help, and only then go to their daughter's house.

And they did so. They reached their daughter's house with the police officers, but were not allowed inside. While the parents spoke to the girl, her husband stood guard.

The girl told her parents that she was three months pregnant. This was the first time her parents came to know of this. She said her in-laws had serious differences with them and would not change. She said that her in-laws were very cranky. Hence, now that she was on her way to become a mother, she had no choice but to do as her in-laws asked her, to buy peace. She also told her parents that she would not be able to keep in touch with them. When the mother admonished her daughter that they had not educated her to surrender in this manner, the girl had no answer. The parents rang me up later and asked me to withdraw the complaint.

It angered me a lot to hear all this. I saw the real state of our so-called educated girls. Many girls like this computer software engineer are under house arrest for fear of losing a place in their in-laws' houses. They are afraid of freedom. The parents are helpless. They resign themselves to forgetting all about their daughters once they are married, and the daughters have to forget their parents.

What use is this education and the so-called modernisation? No wonder, then, that girls are still unwanted in our society. The fault is our own.

14
Pregnant Questions

The audience comprised Fulbright scholars from diverse fields and different regions of the world. The subject of my speech was "Position of Indian Women in Contemporary (Indian) Society". Since the participants were all educationists, I wondered where to begin from. Should I make this an academic session, of which they may have had too many? Or should I make it a realistic and practical class? Also, I wanted to neither overstate nor understate the situation. I wanted to remain authentic to my direct learning and experiences from my career and running of two non-governmental agencies, which included family counselling centres.

It is my belief that a single speaker cannot say it all on a vast topic like this. I could only present a viewpoint which could stimulate and provoke the audience to ask questions. I informed the listeners that the reality, in my opinion, was that the position of an Indian woman in our society was directly dependent on the following situations and questions:

- Where was the girl born and where did she live as a child? Which family was she nurtured in? What kind of parents, grandparents did she have and what were their mindsets? What kind and level of economic status, for availability of resources? Which religion? What caste? How many siblings? Was there a preference for boys prevailing in the family?
- The place of birth? Urban or rural? Forward or backward area? What kind of infrastructure and facilities were available for transportation, education, and training?

- Proximity of schools, how close or far? What kind of schools were available? Kind of teachers? Their mindsets and attitude towards gender issues? The prevailing environment? Knowledge of English? What was the school policy? What kind of school did she study in—missionary, government, or private? Did the girl receive higher education from a school, college, university, or a professional institute?

The position of an Indian woman is undoubtedly influenced by all the above factors and situations. These impact her, just as they impact the boys. But the impact is considerably different for a girl-child or an adolescent, in view of the strong influence all these factors or situations have on her. She is constantly dependent on family and peers for social approvals which, at times, may be unduly restrictive, even to the point of suffocation.

The matter does not end here. Even if a woman—and there are innumerable now—in contemporary India receives the best of all facilities from her parents, there is still a major question of her status in society when she marries. The questions related to marriage are:

- Whom does she marry? How does she marry? With how much does she marry? What kind of a man is he? And the in-laws, most importantly the mother-in-law—who is she? What are her beliefs? How secure or insecure is she? What are her expectations?
- Her husband's expectations: How soon does he desire her to be a mother? And how many times? Does she have a say in it? What kind of financial independence does she have? Does she have full or partial rights?
- What kind of freedom does she have in regard to her own family? Is she in a position to support them in case of need or her own desire to do so?
- Most of all, is she a mother of a son? How many? For that many times she is considered socially secure, with

no reasonable social security schemes in sight yet. For parents in India, and most of all for a woman, sons are the life-long security and what they become as men, add to her status in the society.

> *But the more the status changes, the more it remains the same.*

All these situations place women in the *haves* or the *have-nots* categories. The have-nots are the depressed, dependent, oppressed, controlled, enslaved, supervised, protected, covered, hidden, sheltered, worshipped, abused, used. The haves are the leaders, champions, beacons, thinkers, writers, entrepreneurs, officers, inventors, sarpanch, rulers, goddesses. The difference between the two is, where they were born, who they were nurtured by, and how the circumstances shaped and defined what they wanted. The haves is a growing number, no doubt, and includes more than a million women in our *panchayats*, including the *Pati Sarpanch*—whose husbands rule by proxy.

But the more the status changes, the more it remains the same. The progress gets lost in the increasing population of over a billion, with a skewed sex ratio because of sex-selection, aborting girls before they are born. I have heard many instances of purchase of women by men because there were no women of marriageable age available in their villages. In a society which continues to prefer boys over girls, there will be a need to buy, kidnap, or procure women for marriage. All this is a part of the contemporary Indian society, economic prosperity and higher education notwithstanding.

The fact is that in India a woman is still not an individual by herself. She is a daughter, a wife, a mother, a sister, a daughter-in-law, or a mother-in-law first. The point is that while a woman is all of above, she can be a person too, with an independent status. But not many are there yet—we are not talking of exceptions!

15
To Be Home by Sunset

When we girls were growing up in the 1960s, the instructions from our parents were—be home by sunset. And whenever we got delayed for any reason, I remember the extra care we had to take to reach home safely. I recall many instances when we had encounters with wild-looking men on the prowl. They were there on the roads and by-lanes, on scooters, in cars, and even on cycles. They were young and also not-so-young. In fact, the behaviour of these prowlers taught us self-vigilance, alertness, quick responses, self-protection, and the possible strategies of self-help.

My sisters, our friends, and I grew up in this environment of self-survival, which became a training ground for what it is to be a woman in our society. It prepared us to be conscious of our biological vulnerabilities, while understanding the deficiencies of many a starved male mind. With both realities understood, as women, we had two choices: i) to surrender, limit our mobility, and stunt our growth as women; or ii) accept the reality and fight our way to growth and independence, while taking on the challenges as they came.

And it is exactly this message that I would like to give here. I offer two blueprints for action: one, of self-dependence, self-confidence, and self-defence for women, and the second, a plan of action for the local police, which it ought not to relent on, if women have to be given safer roads and neighbourhoods.

First, for my gender.

Recognise that on the roads, by-lanes, and in public places, just as there are good and responsible citizens going about their duties diligently, there will also be the mentally deficient and physically deprived men who have nothing better to do than ogle at and harass women.

Realise that prevention is better than cure. Hence, do all that you must to prevent situations which make you vulnerable. Do not call for or invite trouble. Use your head more than your heart. Where circumstances become unavoidable, use your instincts and your alertness to get yourself out of the difficult situation. Have courage and remain brave. Showing fear and helplessness makes you an easier victim.

Practise building of physical agility and quick reflexes. For students, sports, NCC, NSS, cycling, outdoor games, and training in martial arts are all exercises in preparation for self-defence. Hence, schools, universities, training institutions, homes, neighbourhoods, residents' welfare associations need to compulsorily train girls in self-dependence and self-defence. And physical fitness should be a habit for all age groups.

Now, for my profession, that is, the police:

There is a need for regular gender sensitisation programmes at all unit levels. There should not be any let-up in this respect. Various training programmes, which are impact making and which deeply impress the mind and the heart, ought to be vigorously given. In such trainings, men and women police officers both should to be present together.

> *As women, we had two choices: i) to surrender, limit our mobility, and stunt our growth as women; or ii) accept the fact and fight our way to growth and independence, while taking on the challenges as they came.*

Regular feedback from men and women police officers on duty and the area's people on the roads and in the neighbourhoods is a must. This will enable the day-to-day deployment to become need-based, save wastage of human resources, and replace the bookish or mere statistical approach.

Deployment, thus, would become strategic once it is based on the ground realities, directly related to observations, dialogue, intelligence, and cross-checking. For instance, the best people to give feedback on their problems are women who work in the night shifts and have to travel by buses, taxis, three wheelers, or their own personal transport. Contact with them on a regular basis will tell us what happens to them on the roads every evening.

I did one such test-check with the nursing staff of a government hospital and they had a large number of tales of woe. They said that at many bus stops where they have to wait for buses, there are also call girls loitering around. And working women going for their duty, who are waiting at the bus stops, are also suspected to be call girls by those passing by. The men hovering around in their cars pass all kinds of indecent comments. There are no policemen around to whom they could complain, and perhaps these loiterers in cars or the call girls are not afraid of the police.

I believe it is possible to know what is happening if intelligent assignment of duties is done. Correct positioning of women police officers in plain clothes could expose these depraved men and get them caught red handed. If this is done as a regular exercise all over the city, the fear of getting caught will increase and rid the roads of these prowlers.

Another necessary check ought to be of the evening buses on the move. They need to be stopped and checked at regular intervals to cleanse them of alcoholics, eve-teasers, and vagabonds. The bus drivers and conductors must expect to be checked at any time, at any place. This will drive home the message that the buses cannot be safe havens for mobile crimes after sunset.

The above are just a few of the many measures which can be taken and followed daily. Based on regular feedback at all police stations, strategies can go on improving and evolving and made more comprehensive and result oriented.

The need of the hour is for relentless, comprehensive preparations and prevention, individually and collectively, to be incorporated as concepts of practical policing. Within weeks, the situation can change dramatically. The headlines in newspapers, then, would be about women who challenged the men who still dared to misbehave. The message to the deranged men would be to look for other means of entertainment as their misbehaviour with women will land them in great trouble. And maybe they would be afraid of the women cops in plain clothes. Also, why would the male police officers not be on duty there if they are regularly sensitised, inspired, motivated, and trained to check, detect, and prevent crime against women?

Both these blueprints are not complicated. They are simple, provided they become a part of the personal growth of women, and the work culture of the police. The results will be tremendous. The roads will be safer and provide free mobility for the women of the city to contribute to its growth and realise their full potential.

But as of today, the instructions which our parents gave us as girls in the 1960s, to return home by sunset, remain valid — even in 2003.

16
Where Women Groan under Bride Price

Is a woman only born to pay the price for being a woman? Will she always be considered a commodity to be passed over to the next person? Or a property to be possessed, transferred, and owned? Or work as a slave for a price already paid for?

Who are we talking about? Not about the kind of women we see and recognise and who escaped all this by good fortune or by sheer determination! We are talking about the vast majority of women all over the world who neither had the right parenting nor the opportunity to learn how to fight the evils in their lives.

The reason why I am unsparing in what I say is based on my recent experience in Africa, where I went for my official work and came across the practice of a custom called bride price. I thought that we, in India, were the worst when we paid, and in many cases continue to pay, the price for groom purchase by paying hefty dowries to the family of the groom.

Here, in Africa, what I saw was the reverse. Here a dowry was paid to the bride's family to possess the bride. Many times the absentee fathers came in at the "right time" to trade and walk away with the daughter's price. Therefore there is, of course, no smothering of girl infants, like in India. In many instances, here it was evident that the parents looked at their daughters as sources of income and demanded too much from the groom's side.

And it is exactly this prevailing custom of bride price which women's groups from across the continent came together to protest. They presented some exceptional individuals to inspire and educate the gathering. For instance, a sixty seven year old women's rights activist and one of Kenya's important politicians, Mrs Wambui Otieno-Mbugua, who is said to be the first Kenyan woman who was in a position to reject the payment of bride price when she was first married. She said she had told her father, to the applause of everyone present at the gathering, "I am your daughter and cannot be bought by anybody."

> *It is possible only when communities seek alternate ways of valuing women and girls—through their skills and abilities, and empower them to contribute to society's development.*

The practice of bride price is a widespread and entrenched cultural tradition in Africa. What started as a token of appreciation that cemented the bond between two families, has gone on to become a method for the accumulation of wealth, with the bride's family routinely demanding a large number of livestock in addition to other presents. The tradition requires the man to give money and goods as well as foodstuffs, and in some cases labour, to the bride's family.

The tradition may vary from country to country and from one clan or tribe to another. But once the groom has paid all that had to be paid, he starts looking at his wife as his property.

The practice of bride price perpetuates the low status of women and keeps them in bondage and abusive relationships. Many young women in these marriages were unable to refuse cohabitation or insist that their husbands protect themselves, which made them vulnerable to HIV or AIDS. "You have been paid for, so how are you able to negotiate in such a relationship?" the women are asked.

Will we ever have "Freetowns" for women? (Freetown, the capital of Sierra Leone, is where, on a historical day, all slaves were freed by the United States; hence the name of the city). Where grooms do not have to be bought and brides are not enslaved by the evil practice of bride price?

Well, it is possible only when communities seek alternate ways of valuing women and girls—through their skills and abilities, and empower them to contribute to society's development. And when governments establish enduring partnerships with non-government organisations to prepare the civil society to agitate for, bring about, and respect change. It basically boils down to the need for enlightened leadership, both in governance and in the voluntary sector.

But, until then, the majority of women across the world will continue to experience hell on earth. So much for the Women's Day that just passed by.

17
Woman, Help Her, Help Yourself

I was at a well-attended women's conference held in Mumbai titled "Women Mean Business", initiated and organised by the Cherie Blair Foundation. Cherie Blair, the wife of the former British Prime Minister Tony Blair, is a powerful woman in her own right. She studied at the London School of Economics, is a barrister and accredited mediator, and an active campaigner of empowerment of women, equality, and human rights issues. Her Foundation brought together many accomplished women from many challenging fields.

They were there at the conference, to hear others and share their own experiences. As I interacted with them, I saw them verbalising an emerging need. It was the need to reinvent the way we work—one which provides for work-family (read children) balance.

The need is to have in-office lactation centres, crèches, long maternity leave, facility to work from home, transfer to a city or place or position of choice, flexible working hours—all to manage the home front. For an Indian woman, and also for women elsewhere in the world, home responsibilities of elder care, child care, children's education, guest support, and even meeting the social demands of her husband, need a lot of energy and time.

A recent news report suggests that every second recruit entering the $60-billion Indian IT industry is a woman. By the time they are in mid-thirties, many of them are reported to be quitting their jobs providing six-figure salaries and foreign travels, to become stay-at-home mothers.

In India, for the first generation of women professionals, there was some home support available through family, especially elders. But no more, for the elders now are busy fulfilling their own needs. Hence, currently, many young working mothers are increasingly dependent on untrained, unsafe, and fast dwindling home-support personnel.

Credible and trained home support is their major need. Many reports suggest that often professional women are forced to choose between a job and home.

So where do we go from here? In the conference, I emphasised the need to fill the vacuum of support through home care services. These also have a strong potential for expanding entrepreneurship, to address each aspect of home management requiring specific skills.

Quality services have become the urgent need of every working woman. In the western world, there are no people available to provide these, except at a very unaffordable cost. Here in India, at least for some years, these can still be available at reasonable prices, in a professional manner at different tiers. This will also replace the system of poor tribal women being "trafficked" at times for such services and left on their own, vulnerable to exploitation.

Keeping in view the range of needs, every working woman can employ more than one woman, who, with the income earned, can provide for their own families in a manner which will make it a win-win situation. But the key question is, who will be the service providers?

The answer lies in a plan for a whole range of home care support services as an industry in areas of elder care, child care, school and home-work management, participation in extra-curricular activities which may include dropping and picking up the child, nutrition and food management, home delivery, laundry services, groceries and other essential shopping, home security, message taking, home maintenance, guest services, mail-desk management, and so on, each requiring a different element of orientation or training. This is what could be given by the service provider at an affordable cost, as a sound business model.

> *Credible and trained home support is their major need.*

This is a multimillion dollar service industry, which awaits enterprising Indian women and men. They only have to establish the right network with allied training centres and then assemble the trained human resource for suitable placements.

There can be linked programmes for young entrants, who are more than eighteen years old and who wish to continue their education but do not have the money to be admitted to open universities. They can work and educate themselves at the same time. Later, they too can become engagers. The economic and social benefits are endless.

Today, one of the biggest employers in the country are the security agencies. Why? Because everyone, home or office, wants security. The levels of requirements may be different, from rudimentary to sophisticated technology driven ones.

It can be the same with home care services. And since this work comes so naturally to women, this ought to be encouraged and incentivised, for the society will get manifold benefits. Home care can be encouraged as an enterprising career option in colleges, since men too would be needed in certain households.

The largest benefits likely to accrue are to the professional women. Indeed, they can help generate an explosion of employment opportunities for other women. By this, women will become job providers for other women.

18
Do You Really Mean Business?

I was invited to speak at an international women's conference on "Doing Business in India". The conference was hosted by a very well-known multinational information technology company having a strong base in India.

The invitation to speak on this topic did cause me some anxiety, in view of the prevailing scenario of corruption and perception of weak governance. My immediate reaction was to decline.

I did not seem to have exciting ideas on promoting business by foreigners in my country. And unless I was personally convinced, how do I inspire outsiders to invest their hard earned money in my country? I did not want to lead them on a garden path. It would be unethical. I could only highlight the existing opportunities and suggest them to explore more on their own.

The hosts also wanted me to share my ideas on how corporate houses could fulfil their corporate social responsibility while doing business in India. They wanted some examples. This requirement was easier to meet. I am aware of several business houses doing excellent work by forging partnerships with non-profit organisations or through their own initiatives.

What was tough and challenging was to identify credible reasons for these prospective women investors to do business in India. And while doing so, not be hamstrung by the many debilitating factors which the Indian community lives with, such as red-tape and corruption.

I literally ransacked my brains to list out convincing reasons for this large group of women entrepreneurs. But I found only limited answers. I could only tell them some things without any misrepresentation. But I could not tell them many other things which are well-known to all of us, for we suffer them in our own ways, by our own creation.

> *We should also factor a budget for giving as a part of our business plan right from inception. If that is done, then it will not feel like profit being lost.*

First, this is what I could tell them:

"Friends, welcome to doing business in India. I can emphatically say that you can always remain in business in India for the following reasons:

1. India has a population of 1.2 billion or 121 Crores. This is equal the population of United States, Indonesia, Brazil, Pakistan, Bangladesh, and Japan put together. So it's a huge demographic resource. You have so many consumers all the time.

2. Around 65 percent of Indians are below the age of 35. There are 600 million under 25 years of age. This is three times the combined population of Britain, France, and Germany.

3. India adds to its population 26 million people, which are equivalent to one UAE or one Singapore or one Australia, every year. Hence there will never be a fall in demand for goods and services which your business may provide.

4. In India, 400 million people are TV viewers. This means there are these many people who are watching what is going on and have aspirations for acquiring goods.

5. According to a recent CII-Kearning report, the Indian luxury industry is expected to grow at 25 percent a year. So here is a 450 million middle class population, and growing, waiting to buy goods. Their consumption will grow with growing incomes.

Having established my case based on the consumer numbers, I moved on to say that it was important that all women in business set new rules of doing business by additions if values, which, in other words, may be termed as "Business Plus". By this I meant that along with business, we should enlarge our activities to care for our consumers. We should also factor a budget for giving as a part of our business plan right from inception. If that is done, then it will not feel like profit being lost. It will become integral to the earnings. The area of giving can be part of the core services or products or whatever is close to the hearts of the founders of the business. For example, those involved in large use of water as a core input could replenish it by water harvesting projects in the same area to ensure surplus recharge; those in information technology could set up learning opportunities for the young and the old who, after a lag period, could become users of the same technology. There are many opportunities for contributing to the society which can be explored. There is no end to creative giving.

Let me now share with you what I could not tell them:

To get skilled resources for their businesses they may have to struggle. India has a vast population of growing unskilled-literate-unemployed. India has only ten thousand vocational schools, compared to China's five hundred thousand. India has less than four hundred universities as compared to Japan's four thousand.

What I could not tell them was there will be many literate-unemployed people, without the skills-sets to meet their needs. Therefore, there will be an extra challenge for them of in-house re-training and then of retaining them.

Ethics demands that before anyone is encouraged to set up business here, they are fully informed of challenges, so that they do business knowingly. This will then make them move from "India incorporated" to "India inclusive".

19
Build Women's Trust in Police

Why don't women report to the police when they are being harassed or intimidated? The recent case of Radhika Tanwar, a student, who was shot dead on her way to college by a person reportedly stalking her for some years, is a case in point.

The general reason given for not reporting to the police is absence of trust. The women complainants are not sure that the police will lodge their report or ensure an effective and sustained follow-up action to stop recurrence.

These apprehensions are not unfounded. The root causes for the lack of trust need to be addressed.

Let me analyse the issue.

First, the prevailing belief is that the police will not lodge the complaint. This belief is correct. Non-registration of complaints is the rule and registration of FIR an exception.

The reason why it happens is that police performance is judged internally by the number of FIRs registered, and not the trust perception of the public. The latter is never objectively evaluated as a tool to measure performance. Registration of FIRs freely and openly will increase the number of crimes in the reports to the seniors and put the juniors on the defensive. Lower numbers provide better perception about efficiency.

This kind of statistics-based mindset needs a wholesale change. Other indicators of police performance which include evaluation of trust have to be put in place.

Second, a common man is not aware about all the options he has concerning reporting crime to the police. He still thinks that going to the police station is the only way. He does not know that informing the police control room by calling 100, sending a written complaint by post or email to police headquarters—as all of them have websites—are also valid processes. The complainants can also keep track of the status of their complaints. It is their right to know the action taken on their case.

Third, another reason why the police avoid recording complaints is that

> *If the police department really wants enhanced security for women, the women must be encouraged to report crime through any of the available means, and feel assured of an effective response.*

every complaint means extra work and expense. Given an option, they lower their burden. Staff is never sufficient to meet the growing pressures of even maintaining law and order. And work of law and order and investigation is not separated, despite clear directions given by the Supreme Court in its judgment in 2006 on police reforms. The same people have to do both.

My view is that if the police department really wants enhanced security for women, the women must be encouraged to report crime through any of the available means, and feel assured of an effective response. This faith will provide useful information to the police to follow up and take timely preventive actions.

Adequate information to police can be a very effective tool for initiating early prevention through appropriate laws and social control. Early prevention means stopping the delinquent from becoming emboldened.

Radhika's murder by a crazy stalker and not having reported the stalking to the police earlier, is a typical example. This crime could have been prevented if she had reported it and it had been effectively followed up. As reports indicate, the stalker had been harassing her for the last three years. Her family and friends knew this, but none of them reported it, perhaps for lack of trust or confidence in the police, or sheer lack of awareness about the options available.

The police department, by encouraging reporting, doing effective investigation, and requesting courts to give only conditional bail to the accused to place the onus on the sureties asking for release of such accused, will check repeat offences and bring in social control. These actions will also go a long way in instilling confidence among women.

The legislators, too, must ensure that where the law is deficient, they step in and legislate suitably, as is the case in "stalking".

And most important of all is to expand the enrolment in Civil Defence services by bringing in the youth, particularly students, as civil defence volunteers. This initiative squarely rests with the respective state governments. They can enrol students for civil defence to perform duties as citizen-cops.

If the police department is short of resources, the civil defence need not be. All the NCC and NSS students can be enrolled as civil defence volunteers to serve the community. And one out of every 100 students could be enrolled to serve in areas of social defence.

The point is that we must use whatever resources we have effectively. By enrolling the youth we will ensure that young students, boys and girls, understand their social responsibility. Imagine, thousands of students of colleges being collectively trained to be members of civil defence! They will all learn of their rights and responsibilities in crime prevention. Will crime not be better prevented and better responded to? And security of women enhanced in the process?

Preparation is prevention. It is the duty of the government agencies to involve the youth to share responsibility.

Government departments do have budgets to provide for such services. Why not invest here, to prevent crime and enhance security?

20
First Ladies, Take the Lead

The real challenge is, how do we make people care? This was a common refrain of a just concluded International Summit held in New York on "Women in World, Stories and Solutions" hosted by Tina Brown, editor-in-chief, *The Daily Beast*. The speakers and participants at the summit were some of the brightest in the world of media, governance, and social engineering. I was happy to be among them.

The collective call for care made me recall a suggestion I had made in an earlier international conference of Arab women leaders on the need to raise issues of care from a position of power, right from the top.

I proposed a caucus of First Ladies around the world to take the lead. The idea was about the synergy created by the high-powered and highly visible, who had influence, contacts, clout, understanding, goodwill, and sensitive social leadership.

Imagine a world where First Ladies would regularly assemble and create meaningful road maps for peace and development; focus on availability of drinking water, health care access, security, and how these were impacting women's mobility and human rights; address issues of education opportunities, gender sensitive and accountable budgeting, and women's representation in governance and the business world.

All such influential women are there, but they are not networked. They are not united enough to work for an equitable world.

I imagined a strong, united forum of First Ladies of Africa, Asia, Americas, and Europe, coming together within their own continents and as "one world" at regular intervals, in different parts of the world, as common citizens, and setting the agenda for the United Nations, the G8, and the Davos, to cite a few forums.

> *Imagine a world where First Ladies would regularly assemble and create meaningful road maps for peace and development.*

In other words, the world needs a First Ladies caucus, comprising the past and the present, to "annex" care-and-concern issues while being on the left or the right of their husbands in political power.

It is time they go beyond their ceremonial roles. Imagine the combined power of the First Ladies. This group will have the power to forcefully change the way we prioritise government policies and compel a change in the way care-and-concern for women is addressed.

The same also applies to the first ladies of the corporate CEOs around the world, as well as other influential bodies and groups.

It will be fascinating to see a summit at an annual General Assembly of all the First Ladies, run in parallel with the UN General Assembly, which decides to exclusively focus on development issues and keep politics out of the door. The world will get together in humanity and prosperity as never witnessed before. It will achieve what the UN today only struggles to.

The western world, after the economic crisis, is suffering from donor fatigue. Any social service project, if conditional to financial aid, remains either non-sustainable or a non-starter. Hence, bringing the First Ladies together is the most visible, effective, and sustainable way of driving change and perhaps showing a new way of doing business.

Another do-able idea to bring out care-and-concern, which I expressed at Tina Brown's summit for everyone's consideration, was to harness the power of media, be it print, voice, or visual. This idea was about the spread and power of information. I proposed that each discipline of media should declare its interest in a particular area of care-and-concern and voluntarily dedicate space to it. This means they could identify and declare areas which are close to their heart, work to keep people interested in their cause, and perhaps even co-opt them for proactive action.

The issues could be numerous, such as environment, gender concerns, children, health matters, research, legal awareness, human rights, globalisation, climate change, law enforcement and the criminal justice systems, democracy, safety, good practices in various areas, community action, and so on. This list is not exhaustive. The point is that the media should offer their resources without charge on issues they choose, to follow up and reach out to the remotest parts of the world through their power of reach.

I foresee that many a media may get identified with the cause they espouse along with their own identity. This will generate curiosity in people interested in the same cause to learn more about the media organisation.

While making this suggestion, I was hoping for just a small bit, to begin with, even if it was a minute a day on TV or radio, or a few inches of space in print media, but on a regular basis. By this process, the media, too, can fulfil its corporate social responsibility.

These ideas, if followed, will certainly make the world a better place for our future generations.

We can begin any time, as this needs no budgets or grants or institutional support. It only needs a caring, innovative, and enlightened willpower.

21
Get Up, It's Your World Too!

Let me begin with some startling eye-openers I came across in the Census 2001 concerning half of our population—women. These are matters of grave concern. Here are these shockers!

Eye-opener number one:

The child sex ratio has been steadily declining in the last 40 years. The ratio of girls per 1000 boys (0-6 years) in 1961 was 976. In 1971 it came down to 964. In 1981 it further reduced to 962. In 1991 it dropped to 945 and in 2001 it went down even more, to a low of 927.

Eye-opener number two:

Sex selection is more prevalent in urban areas than in rural areas. The census result shows that there are 946 girls to 1000 boys in rural areas, as against 900 in urban areas.

Eye-opener number three:

Educated families are aborting girls at a faster pace than illiterate families. The census result of sex ratio at birth with level of education of the mother is 920 girls for every 1000 boys born of the illiterate mothers, as against 876 of graduate and above women.

Eye-opener number four:

Sex selection occurs in all religions. Christians are in the best position with 964 girls for 1000 boys. The Muslims follow them with 950. Buddhists come after, with 942. The number for

Hindus is 925, followed by Jains, with a low of 870. The Sikhs are in the worst situation with a mere 786 girls.

Eye-opener number five:

National averages hide steep declines and critically low ratios in certain regions. The States and the Union territories with the highest decline in child sex ratio are the more well-off ones. Against the national average of 927 girls for 1000 boys in 2001, Maharashtra had 913, Rajasthan had 906, Himachal Pradesh had 897, Gujarat 878, Delhi 863, Haryana 820, Punjab 793, and Chandigarh was shockingly low at 745.

Eye-opener number six:

According to global comparison of 10 most populous countries, India's position is exceedingly embarrassing. The following is the information from the Population Division of the Department of Economic and Social Affairs of the United Nations Secretariat, World Population Prospects: The 2008 Revision. Russia had 1164 girls against 1000 boys, Japan 1053, Brazil 1031, USA 1027, Indonesia 1003, Nigeria 995, Bangladesh 978, and Pakistan 942. India was as low as 936 (2008). China was at the bottom with 927.

As if this was not enough, a survey report of the State of the World Mothers, conducted by an NGO called Save the Children, released just few days ago, says that India is in the unenviable position of being 73 out of 77 middle-income countries. In other words, India is not a safe place to be a mother. India has two-thirds of all the deaths reported for under-five children and maternal deaths in the world.

All these statics establish that while India has a declining girl-child ratio, India is also not a safe place to be a mother. These are the shocking eye-openers one needs to confront and address.

The health of a woman, as the report stated, is closely linked to a woman's educational and socio-economic status. Thousands of women are dying because they cannot access the most basic health care facilities, or if these are available, they are of an abysmal quality.

All this is when Indians worship innumerable goddesses for every bounty on this earth, be it power, wealth, health, knowledge, safety, prosperity, peace, and even reproduction.

This is the height of hypocrisy.

The problem is that in our country all this is inherited and ingrained in the mindsets of men and women from their childhood. And unless this is re-wired, it will hurt the entire society even more in the times ahead. Crimes against women and social violence will increase as there will be fewer women to make a balance in the society. As it is, there are reports of "imported wives" and "shared wives", besides increasing trends in human trafficking.

> *All those who are in a position to change this shocking state of affairs have a moral responsibility to do so.*

There are many laws for these problems, but they are not implemented. When everyone is a violator, who does the police catch? When all give and take dowry, who is a complainant and who is the accused? And where is the evidence to prosecute? And who will depose as a witness and not turn hostile later? With no punishment, the evil has become a common social practice.

One of the major reasons for the preference for a son is the evil of dowry. Or the fear of transfer of property on migration, since a daughter is seen as migratory bird.

All those who are in a position to change this shocking state of affairs have a moral responsibility to do so. And these are mostly parents and men and women in the field of education, positions of leadership, influence, authority, enforcement, and control. Most of all, the youth of India have to act because otherwise their future will be seriously impaired.

We must always remember that an imbalanced society and nation cannot assure harmony, peace, and prosperity.

Be the change you want to see, as Gandhiji said.

22
Giving Asia Women Leaders

Two years ago I was a silkworm that depends on a tree's leaves and is busy whole nights and days knitting its silk. Now I am a watchful butterfly. I am working for a better life for my country and myself. I have horrible memories. My place is a broken ship. And we women travel in that broken ship. I am working to change my grandmother's fearful life, my mother's colourless life, my aunt's unjust life, and my cousin's uneducated life. Today I am like a butterfly opening my wings. I feel the pure wind of the honest morning touching my whole body with joy and I can say words from my mind and heart.

This is what a girl student at Asian University for Women (AUW), Chittagong, Bangladesh, wrote.

Another one wrote:

Two years ago I was a cook for my family. Now I am a daughter to my whole country. Two years ago I was a typical person who went to school and returned home. Now I speak my mind. I'm confident. I analyse the situation. Now I think about my future. I want to represent my people and help them solve their problems.

Another one said:

Our classes help us to analyse the world's problems. This is power through knowledge. Knowledge comes through education. I strongly believe that women's education will solve the problems that our mothers have been suffering through generations and generations.

This university, set up just two years ago, is emerging as the "Harvard of the East" for women. It is exclusively for women and at present has students from over twelve countries, including Pakistan, Afghanistan, India, Sri Lanka, Philippines, Myanmar, Laos, Cambodia, Vietnam, China, and Iran.

The mission statement of the university is "Educating the leaders of tomorrow — today."

> *When women are adequately and correctly educated, they empower societies and build nations.*

The students are selected through coordinators in different regions. Many get full scholarship while some get a partial one for graduate courses. Post graduate courses will be started later. Funding is from USA, individual trusts, and donors.

The University was founded with the primary objective of preparing young women of the region for an "empowered" tomorrow. They are selected from deserving students who are bright and keen to pursue their education, but do not have resources to receive this quality of university education.

I was invited to meet and speak to this group of students under a programme called "Extraordinary women".

I saw a huge confidence in each one of them. In my interaction, I asked them how they saw themselves now, when they visited their homes and met their friends. They gave me a very mature answer. They said, "We now understand why our parents or friends hold on to certain outdated perceptions. Instead of getting into arguments with them, we are respectful of their views, but we are convinced of our own needs to be empowered."

This is huge maturity which these girls are gaining at such a young age.

What I saw was that this university was creating a nursery of women leaders in Asia. These leaders may also spread out all over the world. But the kind of sensitivity they are receiving and experiencing, and the commitment they are developing for their own countries and the region will pull them back to serve where they are most needed.

They are being made conscious of their country and the regional challenges. Their summer vacations, internships, projects, and exposure trips are all focused towards this goal. Full credit goes to their multicultural faculty which is ensuring that the students get the best of the East and the West.

This is an institution where strong regional bonds are being developed amongst over twelve nationalities, in spite of the inherent diversity of history and culture. This is a place of celebration of the Asian continent, unique in all respects. Over the years, AUW will produce broad-minded unifiers, who will resolve regional issues through maturity and understanding. It's a clear investment for the future.

This is the way forward, through the right kind of education. It provides lessons for educational institutions within our own country as well as elsewhere.

In my speech, I left a challenge to the girls to outshine all others in the spirit of giving and building social institutions and prove that when women are adequately and correctly educated, they empower societies and build nations. They unite and invest. They govern and administer as visionaries. They transform and not just transact. They shun violence and encourage peace and harmony. They build the future while addressing the needs of the present.

The Asian University for Women is a role model, the kind needed for both women and men for a secure future.

23
Preventable Pain

As I sit listening, cross examining, and adjudging between two parties in conflict, be it husband-wife, or partners in business, or close relatives, or just friends, in the recently launched true-life television show, *Aap Ki Kacheri*, there are some common lessons emerging, which I believe are worth sharing for everyone's benefit.

In this article, let me address the predominant issues that emerge between husbands and wives.

Almost all the couples who come to *Aap Ki Kacheri* are, in fact, mismatched couples who got married in haste, without any worthwhile or credible verification or background checks on their claimed incomes, or of ownership of house or business or property. Almost all of them have serious constraints of space for the newly-wed. Most are also are suffering from bad habits, poor educational qualifications and are poorly trained and temporarily employed.

Some couples got married without physically seeing each other even once. They proceeded with marriage even when instances of misbehaviour occurred before the marriage ceremony, be it demands for dowry or gifts, or the girl or the boy telling that she or he was being forced to marry, or the man coming drunk on the night of the wedding, or just disappearing. All this because of some one's false *izzat* (prestige) would be lost or the ego of the mother, or the aunt, or the uncle would be hurt! It appears that the marriage was of mothers, uncles or aunts and not these young couple's. No one really looked at the life that these newly married couples would lead and at the legal responsibilities and rights after marriage. And even more, when children, who would need a happy and a safe home, would be born.

In some cases, even on the first night of the wedding, one of the partners did not want to establish any physical relationship. And for months later, the relationship never got consummated. Instead, the marital relations turned into heavy domestic violence of all kinds of bizarre patterns, from being severely abusive towards each other to self-inflicted injuries, or threatening each other's families while still living in the same house. At the same time, the boy's side would become constantly resentful of the girl going to her parents without permission and her family support considered as interference. The girl's side would resent the man for being highly "obedient" towards his own mother or close relatives, aunts, or brothers.

Many of the women who came to the show knew some vocational work like stitching, tailoring, embroidery, beauty treatment, tuition classes, bangle making, home nursing, computers, and so on. But in most of the cases, the husband's family, led by the mother-in-law, did not allow the daughter-in-law to work and earn, even from home, even in situations where shortage of money was a serious issue. She was expected to strictly be a housekeeper (in custody), as this is what she was brought for.

And this was often the cause of the violence—not working, not obeying, or not serving. The complaints against the women were: demanding money to meet the cost of food articles for her child or her own essentials, wasting money, and also visiting her parents too often for comfort. On being asked why the visits were so frequent, the women asked, where else could they go?

Invariably, the parents were supportive of their daughters, just as the boy's parents were of their sons, even when the sons were admittedly indulging in many vices like coming home drunk, pornography, gambling, and even drugs. The girl's parents were openly regretful of their haste in getting their daughters married, cutting short their education, vocational training, and jobs they were doing.

On the husband's side, I saw almost no remorse in the family over getting their sons married even when they were not financially independent.

Women in India, breaking free from their shackles, may be visible in some places. But there is another bigger reality of a huge mass of them being in pain—needless and preventable pain. It's about insecurities, inadequacies, controls, suspicion, and unpreparedness for the most important event of one's life—marriage. Marriage is still considered as just one more episode in life. Huge loans are taken, by both the boy's and the girl's side, to make this event happen, which further causes stress after marriage.

> *Our society is living under needless fear born out of ignorance, haste, immaturity, and greed. All these problems are preventable, provided we are willing to learn.*

Children too continue to be born, even when nothing is working in the marriage. Boys are preferred over girls. Abortions are done when they suspect that the unborn may be a girl. At times, the woman is expected to bear a child soon after marriage, without giving her any time to settle down in her new environment.

No one is concerned. The couple do not have any forums to go to which provide quick redressal. They are ignorant of their legal rights and responsibilities. They have no one to explain anything to them. There are only myths and fears. Their elders spread ignorance further.

Our society is living under needless fear born out of ignorance, haste, immaturity, and greed. All these problems are preventable, provided we are willing to learn. This is what *Aap Ki Kacheri* endeavours to do. It is more than a TV show. It is creating awareness which results in pain-prevention.

24
Women Sarpanch as Rubber Stamps

Through our rural project, we invited a large number of village women for a dialogue. Our aim was to explore the possibilities of initiating a training programme for the women *panchayat* members in the villages in which we were working. Among those present in the meeting were the elected women panch and sarpanch, besides ordinary residents.

We were looking forward to a rejuvenating and learning experience of hearing the views of the elected representatives of the villagers, women who had the courage to stand up and be counted. Our interaction with them gave us new insights. It made us realise the ground realities and home truths. Here are some excerpts from our conversation:

Q.1 How do you all feel as elected members of the village council?

A: Nothing. There is nothing to it. We are mere rubber stamps. Our men come with the papers and we merely put our thumb impressions on them. We sit apart in the *panchayat* meetings, covering our faces, and feel shy about saying anything.

Q.2 Why do you do this?

A: Because they are men! They control it all. We have no say. Nobody listens to us. And our opinion does not matter anyway. Our men just put us up for elections due to the reservations. And we accept it. After all, they are the ones to decide for us. And it is all right by us.

Q.3 Do you, as women, not let them know that this is not right? And that you would like to exercise your own responsibility?

A: How can we do this? We have no power to tell them. They will never care to listen to us.

> **We women ourselves are each other's biggest enemies. We are always fighting among ourselves.**

Q.4 What about all you women? If you all get together, can you not exercise influence?

A: We are all divided. Actually, we women ourselves are each other's biggest enemies. We are always fighting among ourselves — daughter-in-law versus mother-in-law, sister-in-law versus daughter-in-law. The men, in fact, are quietening us down in our fights. We are also more worried about our household duties, tending to the cattle and the fields, and ensuring that there is enough water, grain, and fodder stored in the house. The men are busy politicking, entertaining each other, and gossiping. But they rule over us because we are always going to them with our problems and they take advantage of this fully.

Q.5 So what do you think is the way out? Is there any hope for you women to play your roles in village management?

A: Yes, we need to be educated. We need to know how to deal with each other. But most of all, women will have to support women, and not be adversaries as they are at present. Why do you not tell us what we should do?

Q.6 Will you come to this centre once a fortnight for an awareness programme?

A: Yes, if you send us the bus again, as you did this time. (they giggle)

We all agreed to meet once every fifteen days. Accordingly, we planned a programme for them called the *Shubchintak* (well-wisher) project. More than forty women came. We began by showing them the map of our country and asked them to tell us what they thought it was. They said it was a picture of a dead cow!

The questions and answers, and the subsequent interaction, made us realise that all *panchayat* training must begin with comprehensive women's education, where they realise for themselves the reasons for their slavery.

What is of concern is whether their men will allow this. Perhaps the first batch of women will have to suffer a backlash. We, as supporters and community workers, saw how gigantic the task was. But then if we, as a nation, are to realise our full potential, the issue of women's education has to be addressed, house to house, and village to village.

25
Women, Seize the Day!

Almost every organisation across the country is preparing to celebrate Women's Day in the first week of March. This is a strong indication of growing awareness of the need to build on inherent strengths of women to ensure a progressive society.

The latest government announcement of the Cabinet approval of Women's Reservation Bill 2008 that seeks to reserve 33 percent seats for women in Lok Sabha and State Assemblies is a step in this direction.

My analysis indicates a rapidly changing role of women in reproduction, production, and community leadership. The scale and speed of change will vary depending on the upbringing and the opportunities available to a particular girl.

First, on reproduction. The major change, as has happened in the West, will be when most women will not marry by default but by considered choice. They will not accept anyone "good enough" as decided by their elders, but wait for Mr Right.

This implies that, gradually, the number of unmarried women will increase. So will marriages be delayed? Will there be fewer children in a marriage? Will the demand for surrogate mothers increase from women who want to have children but also want thin waist lines and engaging careers?

There will be a booming market for the home care industry. Husbands will have to pitch in support in home management. They will not be able to get away saying they are on a fourteen-hour job, because so will women be!

For Muslim women, becoming a second wife may become less acceptable. They will increasingly invoke the less utilised provision of *talaq-e-tafweez* which is a conditional *talaq*, sought on the grounds of husband remarrying, indulging in cruelty towards her, or not maintaining her properly.

There could also be an increase in the acceptability of live-in relationships. This is already recognised under Domestic Violence Prevention Act 2005.

Second, on production. The career growth of a woman will depend on the value addition she makes to her work place. The meeting schedules would shift from the current "over a drink" to "over a coffee".

I believe that the society will see more women in recruitment panels. There is already a government direction to have women in panels when recruiting more than ten persons. This will see more women getting selected naturally. Currently, there are only about 10 percent women employees in the Union Government and fewer still on the boards of private companies, with a mere 4.9 percent of nearly 4,000 companies listed on the stock exchange having women directors.

The Indian society is likely to see more women in decision making positions. This will counter the cliché, "When a man is decisive, he is dynamic; when a woman displays the same firmness, she is difficult." This will be replaced by "When she is firm, she is tough."

At work places, instead of becoming hard taskmasters and trying to compete, women may try to teach some of their better skills to men—soft skills and multitasking.

As Margaret Thatcher once said, "If you want something said, ask a man; if you want something done ask a woman." This may well happen more often.

In search of fresh talent, employers have realised that organisations having gender diversity at all levels are more likely to succeed than those which do not. Women leaders are known to have a participative style of management, which inspires everyone to do well. They are also tolerant of requirements of their team members for family time.

The truth is that in all places, be it home or work, deductive as well as inductive reasoning is needed. Research shows that women's brains have 10 percent more white tissue which enables them to have higher assimilation and intuition. Men's brains have more grey matter which facilitates better processing and enables them to have focused and compartmentalised functioning. Work situations need complementary skills and hence need the synergy provided by both men as well as women working together.

> *In search of fresh talent, employers have realised that organisations having gender diversity at all levels are more likely to succeed than those which do not.*

Third, on community. Moving to the world of community leadership, around ten lakh women elected in India's over six Lakh *panchayats* (village councils), are changing, and will further change, the face of rural India. The first generation of illiterate women leaders is now giving way to the literate ones, who will make a difference in the coming years. The proposed presence of 170 elected women in Parliament, coming "not by inheritance but inherent skills" will also be a harbinger of change. The country awaits this revolution and transformation. The decades ahead belong to the performance of the women leaders.

With this, the onus to perform is squarely on the women. They must perform with integrity and win the trust, in the service of the nation.

26
The Journey to Fearlessness

Invited to speak on fearless leadership, I was expected to recall fearless acts of known or unknown leaders. Instead, I thought I would share the way mother eagles push their young ones out of their nests, perched high up in the trees, only to make them realise who they really were. The young eagles, thrown out of their comfort zone, soon discover the power of their wings as they fly and soar.

Looking at the large audience of young men and women, all above eighteen years of age, in a management school in the interiors of South India, I started to wonder if they, too, were heading for that final push or launch. And were they ready? What about their fears? Have these been addressed? Most of all, how much did they know of the strengths of their own wings?

And so, where should I begin? Do I tell the students the concept of fear and the success stories about conquering it? Or do I trigger their thinking to help them understand and identify their own fears and how to resolve them? And discuss the impact unaddressed fears can have on them and their areas of responsibility, when they reach leadership positions in their professions?

I sensed that this aspect of leadership was probably not taught at the management school. Due to this, several students may be living with fears which will stay with them when they occupy positions of leadership. I was also not sure if they were aware that leadership is felt personally before it can be expressed externally. And fears are internal till exposed.

In my speech, I told them that they were already leaders as individuals, but perhaps nurturing several fears within them. And if not resolved, these fears will grow and always impact their lives, no matter what position they may reach. It is possible that the placement or appointment agency, or competitive examination agency may not be able to detect their fears.

> *They must identify their fears, find the causes, analyse their rationale, and think through the possible ways to deal with them.*

But one day the fears will be exposed, when faced by challenges which will come their way. For instance, one fear which makes several people compromise their principles is the fear of failing to provide for their families.

I started to engage with the students and asked them whether they were aware of what their fears were. They were left thinking. To help them open up, I decided to begin with my own story.

I asked them to guess what could have been my fears when I was their age. Interesting guesses came—marriage, society, insecurity, dowry, parents. I told them that none of these were my fears. I said my fear was the one which probably is and has been the fear of every woman in the world—being dependent, financially or psychologically, on others. In positive terms, I needed to fight this fear and become self-reliant.

I then explained how this fear got translated into effort for achieving total self-discipline and hard work, to be self-reliant, to use every opportunity which came my way, be it in academics, sports, extra-curricular activities, or family support. The biggest opportunity was my service in the Indian Police Service. And Anna Hazare's anti-corruption movement is the latest.

I was driven to ensure that I should be self-dependent. I wanted to be an equal partner and a self-reliant person, who owned responsibility and was in charge of herself. At any time, while sharing, I did not want to lose my space and get overruled, because being a woman I was expected to be soft. I wished to be a provider, equally, like a man is expected to be. This was the reason why I was among them. I became whatever I am today because I dealt with my fear early on. And my family helped me.

Now I started to receive responses from the youth in the form of questions. They bordered around family, society, acceptance, fear of failure, interference, criticism, and so on.

I made them realise that actions on fears cannot be postponed. They must identify their fears, find the causes, analyse their rationale, and think through the possible ways to deal with them. They should take help if they need, take wise and credible counsel, and read about successful people to learn from their lives.

Fears do not disappear by wishing them away. Suppression will merely carry these insecurities and fears to the daily life. You may appear brave, bold, and courageous, but actually, when the time for challenge comes, you will crumble professionally or in personal life. No management or other education is complete without learning to make your own toolkit of dealing with internal insecurities.

Fearless leaders are not born but are self-made. An insecure person merely puts on a façade of leading. Actually, he merely marks time and in the process makes everyone lose too! We see this in the governance of our country today. We can learn from it.

27
A Bunch of Keys

I was recently invited to speak at an event which was full of young women business leaders. They were addressed as Young FICCI or YFLO. All of them had resources to go right to the top of their businesses. They were born in homes which were already well established business houses and renowned names in India and abroad. They were all well groomed and truly inspired.

As I was the keynote speaker, I decided to give them all a "bunch of keys".

Key One: Plan your career

Explore what you want. Then plan it. Plan the next year, two years, and then five years. Look ahead and imagine where you want to be. You must also know how much and how far you are going to work. By doing this, the rest of the priorities in life will weave around and find their own space. But if you fail to plan properly, then you will muddle through, lose time and resources, and may even fail in your goals.

Key Two: Incubate your talent

It's worthwhile to offer to learn to acquire the skills or knowledge. And learn to rise step-by-step while climbing the ladder. This will test your fitness, stamina, commitment, and willpower. Incubation would mean learning to work at the bottom, being a subordinate, and willingness to learn from more experienced persons. And perhaps learning from the mistakes and the right decisions of others.

Key Three: Continuous education

Get as much education as possible. Never stop training and educating yourself. There are any number of distance learning programmes you can enrol in. If employed, continue to show keenness to train and learn.

Key Four: Befriend technology

Use information technology to the maximum. Be a surfer. Which means research and search on the internet. Know about the latest technology as much as possible. Be current with the latest trends in your area of work.

Key Five: Communicate

Develop interpersonal and communication skills. Train to communicate. Learn the art of using the right language and expression. Learn to understand and manage diversity and heterogeneity.

Key Six: Network

Women, too, like the men, must network among themselves as professionals and as friends. Often women at work do not network enough. They finish their work and rush home as they have the additional responsibilities waiting for them there. Or they are too exhausted by the end of the day to even talk, leave alone go out of home. The consequences of not networking are there to be seen. When it comes to the final decisions, women get left out, many times because of the absence of a lobby. And who knows this better than me!

Key Seven: Get wise counsel

Find a mentor. A mentor is not for crying over the shoulder, but one to share your issues with. And clarify your thoughts and bounce off your ideas. You need to have someone you can trust to seek wise counsel.

Key Eight: Be confident

Project yourself with confidence. Do not understate, nor overstate. Take due credit for your bright ideas and good work. There is nothing wrong in letting others know of your achievements, potential, and strengths.

From this bunch of keys I moved on to the three different kinds of pressures women need to understand to make a success of themselves.

First pressure:

Your job will be the same as that of men. You have to produce the same kinds of results. You have to be prepared to deal with this on equal terms.

> *You have to find a balance between personal and professional lives. It is this balance which will either allow you take-off with success or get you grounded.*

Second pressure:

Being a woman, it will bring along attendant stresses such as being particularly visible, excessively scrutinised, and expectations of being a role-model.

Third pressure:

You have to find a balance between personal and professional lives. It is this balance which will either allow you take-off with success or get you grounded. Most people expect that women will take greater responsibility in the family. Beyond the sheer size of such demands, the roles and expectations in the two spheres of home and professional life are often at odds. For example, being business-like and efficient, maybe even tough, at work and warm, caring, and nurturing at home.

Interestingly, research from the Centre for Creative Leadership points out that trying to break through the glass ceiling presented women with even tougher obstacles. They often hit the wall! This keeps them out of the top positions like the head of the corporation. So be aware.

Finally, I talked about being "givers" in education, as a corporate social responsibility. This is education not only of girls, but of boys as well, since most of the avoidable suffering and deprivation which women are going through is a direct result of the negative mindset of males. I have a number of such cases coming up in my television serial *Aap Ki Kacheri*.

If we, as a society, have to be truly progressive, it cannot be men and women at the cost of one another. We have to develop together. Not to be super human beings, but being "superbly human".

It's all about the right bunch of keys.

28
Women Leadership on Test

What are your expectations from the fifty nine women members of Parliament elected to the Lok Sabha this time? This was the question I posed on the weekly radio show I do every Friday on FM radio, Meow, in Delhi.

Since it is a dial-in radio programme, I asked for the views of the listeners. Here are some interesting responses that came in.

The first caller was a teacher in a primary school. She made a great observation. She said that she wanted the elected leaders to ensure that all government schools, which start only from class one, to instead begin with nursery and kindergarten as a preparation for the standard one class. This is what most private schools do.

She said that children in government schools, coming in without this preschool learning, remain at a disadvantage throughout. Class one is not about basics, but starts with reading and even includes poems. Children are expected to be able to read and write the alphabets and small words. In the private schools, these basics are taught in nursery and kindergarten. In the government schools, by the time the teachers teach these basics, they are already halfway through the year and the course of class one becomes pending.

In view of the current policy not to fail children up to class eight, the children keep getting promoted without actually passing the classes. So, in the end, we have children who only struggle along, but actually do not pass. And the results of the school remain poor. Most of the children would naturally like to drop out, not because of poor teaching, but because of the poor start. Most children cannot recover from their initial handicap of not learning and non initiation of their studies either at home or in a play school.

This made good sense. For, in our voluntary organisation, we see this actually happening everywhere. This is why we, in Navjyoti Foundation, run *balwaris* (nursery classes) and KG classes for slum children and those in the villages. And to meet the needs of those who are older, we also run *school ke baad schools*, which are "schools after school" to help children with their homework.

The young children, with weak basics, come to Navjyoti school after their regular school to do their homework under the guidance of teachers. They are the first learners in their families and do not have help at home to catch up. In *school ke baad school* they learn the basics, while in the regular school they proceed with the class course. What an irony indeed! And how unfair for these children that they have to cover the handicap due to elders' neglect in providing for their needs. They lose out in life not because they do not have talent but because someone is not thinking for them.

The caller also pointed out the shortage of teachers in schools and the high ratio of students per teacher. Due to this, the learning environment is very crowded.

This was the teacher's priority for the new elected representatives, especially the women members of Parliament.

Other callers wanted implementation of laws and policies already in place, but not implemented according to expectations. The callers were not asking for anything new, but only wanting the existing laws and policies to be implemented properly. They wanted strengthening of judicial infrastructure, in particular.

But what surprised me was a call from a police officer's wife. She wondered if these women parliamentarians would consider ensuring that police officers have some time for their families. She complained that her husband was never off duty. He was a sub inspector and was always on the job. Their child rarely got to see his father.

Her view was supported by many other callers who said that police officers' welfare, particularly from their family's point of view, should be considered. They suggested formation of a police personnel wives association, on the lines of the army wives welfare association which does so much good work for the rank and file and has large resources to help and care for the armed personnel.

> *Callers wanted implementation of laws and policies already in place, but not implemented according to expectations.*

The most interesting idea, and related to family welfare, was the institution of WEP (Women Entrepreneur Programme) for women in police families. Women who stay at home keep waiting for their husbands to return and, in the process, waste a lot of their time. To use this time better, there could be creative programmes based on their skills and supported by training and marketing. With families beneficially occupied, it will lead to multiple benefits for the society as a whole.

Basically, the callers were hoping for creative solutions to pressing issues which remain festering and eat into the vitals of people's lives.

Will the newly elected be different from their predecessors? Will they remain close to people who have voted them to power? Will they remain grateful for the positions and privileges they have gained by virtue of people's trust?

Only time will tell.

29
Needed Many More Millions

The women's day celebrations have just gone by. We have highlighted strengths of womanhood as well as the challenges we face in society concerning half of our humanity. We have talked of why we need to invest equally in this mass of humanity. We have realised that to have a fully developed world, each individual matters. Each individual contributes to the health and wealth of the nation and the society.

Then why have we taken so long to understand this basic, essential, fundamental concept? Why have we held back women all through history, barring the short phases in ancient times when they are believed to have enjoyed better and equal opportunities? Why have we deliberately kept them as a weaker gender? Why have we restricted them to remain inside their homes? Why have we not created an environment of financial independence for them? Why did we take so long to give them property rights? And how many women really know they have this right? And how many will get it? Why do we make them lose their identity on marriage? Why do we still tolerate dowry taking and dowry giving? How often do women have to fight to even get their *istri dhan* back? Why do we spend more on our sons' education and nutrition as compared to daughters'? Why do we celebrate, barring exceptions, the birth of a son as compared to a daughter? Why does a woman need permission to support her parents in need when she can do so from her own resources? Why is it that one often hears that her salary is to be handed over to the in-laws and she just gets her bus fare? Why is a woman's wage lower than that of a man for the same work? Why is a woman in certain sections of society repeatedly pregnant?

All this is because she is weak. Physically weak; emotionally dependent; economically poor; owns no property; has no identity; leaves behind her own relationships and moves to another house to start life all over again. She is physically vulnerable; gets emotionally related to her children because she gives them birth; children then become her priority; she subjugates her own needs to those of her family; as age advances she is totally dependent on her family to protect her and provide for her. And who is that family? The sons and the daughters-in law.

> *To have a fully developed world, each individual matters. Each individual contributes to the health and wealth of the nation and the society.*

So, then, why will a woman want daughters? Daughters go away. And they go away at a huge cost. And they themselves are dependent on their own families. So why will a daughter's birth be welcome? Which parents will be happy?

Only those parents who believe in equal worth. Those who believe in human dignity; those who value life; those who are secure within themselves; those who are not impatient to shed their responsibility; those who value education over gold and diamonds; those who do not see the society in terms of gender; those who do not want their daughters to lose out the way they did; those who believe in giving decision making capacity to their children, especially their daughters; those who believe in self-reliance, self-respect, self-dependence, having mobility, giving space, courage, and most of all, equality.

Who are these people? They are parents, grandparents, uncles, aunts, and most important of all, teachers.

The first eyes the girl child, after her birth, looks into are her mother's eyes. What do these eyes say? Is she welcome? Is she her love? Then she looks into her father's eyes and those of her grandparents. Is she welcome? All the time she hears being compared to others in the house. Is she a liability or an asset? She hears and she sees. And she feels and she conditions herself accordingly. She rebels or she falls in line.

She now goes to school. She sees and hears. Boys play and she watches. Why? Why can she not play and compete and lose and win? Boys walk to the school alone, but the girl child is always accompanied by someone. Boys tease her and she cries. She holds back out of fear of being teased or assaulted. And her life alters drastically.

We need a whole new generation of forward looking parents. Parents like mine. Who did this all for us. We were not one or two. We were four daughters. They invested in us through our continuous education. They were not worried about their old age. They were worried about us, as to what we would become. They told us of the pitfalls of dependence. They depicted the joys of responsible independence. They taught us the value of books over gold ornaments. They made us mobile. They made us teach a lesson to the boys who teased us. They taught us the value of our time. They taught us to take decisions and take risks. They taught us what it is to be self-respecting. They taught us the difference between giving and asking.

My parents were from a simple town, Amritsar. And there are millions of their kind. But we need many more millions.

30
Neutralising Man-Made Imbalances

They were young men in a vocational class. "You are all learning these trades at this polytechnic school, not to ask for more dowry from your prospective brides. You are learning to support your families better and be self reliant," I reminded them. "But where are even the women to ask for dowry, madam?" Their response made me aware of the reality which we hear and read about all the time. I was in a village in Rajasthan, two hundred kilometres from Jaipur.

I asked the class of boys, "How many sisters do you have?"

"None."

"And brothers?" Almost all hands went up saying, "Plenty and mostly unemployed."

I now moved to the girls who were there to learn skills which would enable them to work from home. Before I could ask them any question, they asked me one. This was from a group of young girls, among many others who were in their late teens, fully covered in black veils. I could only see their eyes. They asked, "What can we do from home? Our parents do not let us go out. This training school was a rare permission for us."

I hesitated for a moment before replying. Within me, I wanted to see these young girls become as free as I was, free from any constricting veils. They seemed to be circumscribed by the insecurities and perhaps the beliefs of their parents and elders. I searched for the right words which would not be misunderstood. I asked them why they could not ask their parents to let them be more visible like their other friends who were also sitting there, and also be more mobile. I realised how truly they were enslaved.

My questions got no answers. I only got wondering looks. Their situation left me with very difficult options. They needed someone to teach them to be a self help group or SHG, which can be linked with procurement, production, and marketing of their goods. But who will handle all this? Who will teach them to be an SHG? Where could they form a group of about ten to fifteen members? They could stitch, tailor, and embroider and someone could market for them, in view of their captivity. They could collectively save, take loans on very low interest rates, and earn money for themselves.

How much could I explain in just one short session? They needed to be made aware, educated, and mentored. This is when I felt the dearth of more catalysts in the form of NGOs and proactive government officials.

The interaction brought in still more questions. The next one from the girls was, "How do we deal with dowry demands?" All the boys present laughed. I said, "When women are scarce in number, why must they still need to give dowry? It's now a case for reverse dowry." But my point hardly registered with them. The whole system of women and dowry is so deeply rooted that the idea of men giving dowry was certainly a joke.

This occasion was when I learnt that the shortage of women for marriage was compounded by the fact that many of the girls, who had educated themselves, were not accepting anyone less educated than them. Men were left behind!

As I drove back, I saw miles and miles of barren land. I wondered why trees had not been planted there. Why was each monsoon season not used to plant millions of trees? Why was this huge youth population not associated with community responsibility? Where were the *panchayats*? Why were all *panchayats* only comprising the old and the retired? Where was this huge number of rural youth? Unemployed and looking for a bride with a dowry price and now not getting it? Will they ever think of being *panch* when they are young and full of issues to be resolved?

I had asked a question of the rural youth present before me during my earlier question-and-answer session, as to how many of them had ever planted any trees? Only a few hands came up.

"What about the others?" I asked. "Do you not use water and eat fruits and enjoy the benefit of trees planted by others?" They all nodded. "Where, then, is your contribution?" I asked.

> *The shortage of women for marriage was compounded by the fact that many of the girls, who had educated themselves, were not accepting anyone less educated than them.*

Every drop of rain matters today. Does this not require a huge community awakening for collective responsibility? Does it not require planting trees on a war footing, involving the entire billion plus population of the country? Can we not plant millions of trees each year?

Must we wait for our elected leaders to lead? Have we not lost time already? Why should we wait? Are we all not leaders in our own right? Should we not take individual and collective responsibility to do the maximum we can? Maybe, then, the imbalances caused by man will be neutralised.

31
Eating the Elephant

Women in police made history a couple of years ago. The rank-and-file came together at a national conference, held in Delhi. It took fifty-four years as an independent India to do so. The conference was the result of more than two years of collaborative hard work by the British Council; the Bureau of Police Research and Development (Ministry of Home Affairs); and the respective host partners like DGPs of Punjab, Andhra Pradesh, West Bengal, and Madhya Pradesh. There were also young women in the Indian Police Service, namely Rina Mitra, Anita Punj, Charu, Malini, Tejdeep, Siridevi, and a few others who played a key role in training the women in police. The coming together was a grand discovery.

When I say women in police made history, I mean it in more than one sense. First, they came together, vertically and horizontally, that is to say across all ranks totalling around 350, and converged without the rigid hierarchy and traditional mindsets. Almost 94 percent of the delegates were from non-gazetted ranks. Only four per cent were women from the Indian Police Service.

This was history because such an intensive vertical interaction for a three-day conference, where all ranks converged and listened to each other as equals, is unusual for the culture of police service in our country. At least, I had not seen anything of this kind in my thirty years of service. This is perhaps because men are traditionally very hierarchical. Without casting aspersions, this has been the mindset. Men in the police service are habituated to an inflexible system of command and control. Not often do the seniors participate and listen. Exceptions, of course, are there.

The second reason for this being a historical event was that the same Vigyan Bhavan in Delhi where the conference was held, has traditionally been the venue for two conferences — the Annual Directors General of Police conference and the Inspectors General of Police conference. One is hosted by the Intelligence Bureau and the other by the Central Bureau of Investigation. This was the first time that the majority of junior ranks sat on the same chairs, in the same hall, and on the same dais as their own Home Minister. The Hon'ble Minister, Shri L. K. Advani, heard them all, and the women in police, in turn, heard him. There was a great deal of warmth, colour, and interaction, which does not happen in the DGP conferences. I am a witness now to both, and can say this from experience.

> *They had never thought they could come together, speak up for themselves, and raise issues for a legitimate role in national security.*

The third reason for the event being historical was that never ever had women in police come together in any manner. And here they came, from different regions across the country. They had never thought they could come together, speak up for themselves, and raise issues for a legitimate role in national security. Interestingly, many had travelled out of their states for the first time.

The fourth reason for this being historical was that all of them came together after having participated in the regional conferences and a three month long Personal Development Programme, conducted for them by their own women officers in the Indian Police Service. It was organised by the British Council, through a British based and internationally renowned training group called Spring Board Inc.

The fifth reason for making history was that the women in police now collectively voiced what they needed. It had taken them so long to even say that they needed separate toilets and resting rooms in the police stations, or crèche facilities in the police colonies. They collectively made it known that they were "being held back" and were being "marginalised" in the posting policy. (Reference: survey findings by Jaya Inderson, an eminent social scientist.)

The sixth reason was that the women in police decided to give themselves a voice by making a forum for themselves, which will keep them knit together hereafter. An Interim Forum was announced and formed.

The wonderful part was also that the Home Minister, Shri L. K. Advani, witnessed this history being made and said he felt honoured to be a part of it. Recognising the power of convergence, he fully supported the effort and said the conference ought to be an annual event, at par with the high profile DGP conference. By this, he gave respect to the need to give women in police their due place.

One of the major highlights of the conference was the presence of the Chief Superintendent of British Police, Suzette Davenport. She elaborated how the women in police in Britain had covered a long distance and were now setting gender agendas for the whole service. They had organised themselves as British Association of Women Police and included sensitive men in their association as well. She said that all this was the vision of one woman constable, Tina Martin, who initiated the whole movement decades ago.

Suzette said, "Remember, my friends, you are at a stage where we were in the 1960s . . . when we knew we were up against an elephant and decided to eat it."

She was joined by Jenny Daisely, the trainer from Spring Board Inc., who said, "Remember to eat it bit by bit."

I added, "Begin with the tail."

And she responded by saying, "See that while you do, the elephant does not soil you or kick you."

To which there was the response, in a chorus, from the audience, "No more. We are today trained to bite the elephant."

Some visible and vocal history was made, just in time for the Women's Day.

32
Parents like Mine

The male personal assistant I have in my house has two small daughters, aged nine and seven. He has lived with us as a family member for over a decade. In fact, when he came to us, he was married but did not bring his wife along with him. Perhaps, then, he did not have the economic means to start a family. Later, he did. Both his daughters are athletic and full of energy. Probably due to our vigilance and subtle pressure, he sent them to a good school that charged a reasonable tuition fee. After paying their fees, he is left with less than half his salary. This makes him feel very insecure. He loves his children, but remains in doubt over what is more important—saving money or spending on their education. Due to our presence, so far, he has not risked taking them out of school. But I know that the day he is on his own, he most likely will.

But I am not writing this to talk about his financial-education dilemma. I am doing so to point out a fundamental truth which struck me the other day, when I saw one of the two girls holding a long stick in her hand and using it to hit a big, deflated ball. She was playing in our garden. I stood there watching her. I saw, then, the drastic difference between her childhood and mine.

I was given a tennis racquet and a whole enabling environment to learn to play and compete. I recall that, at her age, my parents had ensured that straight from our school in Amritsar, my younger sister Reeta and I would go for tennis coaching. My mother would be there, waiting for us, with hot milk and fruits. My father would be there to ensure our proper training. On and off the tennis court, we were guided, motivated, and inspired to become champions. We all shared a vision to succeed and be winners.

It all began when I was about the same age as the daughter of my personal assistant who was playing with a stick and a big, deflated ball. She too wants to be a champion and has the same potential as I had. She is athletic and diligent. But she does not have what I had—the right environment and opportunities, which came through my parents.

In her case, her father was not even sure whether his financial security was more important or his daughter's good education. Her mother works as a domestic help. Despite the fact that the National Stadium is not far from my house, she has no initiative to take her daughter even to a government sports facility. She is also not literate. She has no motivation to educate herself or learn a vocational trade, even though the facility for such training is nearby. This would have enabled her to supplement her family's income. But, no.

In the case of these small girls, the additional misfortune is that their father even uses his financial situation as an excuse to disappear and get drunk once in a while. The wife and children do not know where he is the whole night. In our case, our parents would not sleep till we had gone to sleep.

When I look at these girls, I see the Hand of God—or the Hand of Nature. Who decides to which parents and which home will a child will be born? Who decides what kind of parents a child will get? Till a certain age, I was dependent on the environment created by my parents, just as these girls are. But what a world of a difference! What have these girls done to deserve such a home, and what had we done to get such caring parents? As I watch her play, I wonder about this and seek some answers.

Becoming parents is the biggest responsibility of human beings, for which there is no prior education, no training, no awareness programme, no accountability, no standards, no guidelines, no rules, no orders, and no laid down duties.

It is only the fate of the child which determines what she (or he) gets in the formative years, and once these are over, the impact is forever. Then, when the child becomes an adult, what does she do with what she received? Diminish it, neutralise it, or maximise it? But what remains unexplained is why children like these girls are born to parents who are insecure, unreliable, and perhaps unworthy?

These are the mysteries of life which remain unresolved, undiscovered, unfathomed, and least understood by us ordinary mortals. Imagine, if we had the correct answer, what would the world be like! Maybe, the children of the world could then choose parents like mine.

> *Becoming parents is the biggest responsibility of human beings, for which there is no prior education, no training, no awareness programme, no accountability, no standards, no guidelines, no rules, no orders, and no laid down duties.*

33
Responsible Parenting

A villager in Odisha sold his six-year-old daughter, Hema, to a fellow villager, Ramprasad Mangaraj, a money lender, to pay off a small debt of less than ₹ 3,500. The deal was complete, with a written document that states the girl's status as "adopted" and not "bought". Despite having nothing to eat, the villager, named Shyam Lal Tandi, of Kundabutla village in the Bongomunda block of Bolangir in Odisha, was the father of four children, the fourth being just three months old. Bolangir is facing one of the worst ever droughts which has rendered its poor even more vulnerable. Shyam Lal says that he has no regrets about selling his child. He says that at least that one child will have a more secure life. Lalita, the mother of little Hema, says, "We faced many difficulties, we had to sell her off." When asked, if faced with a similar situation again, would she sell off another child, she replied with tears streaming down her cheeks, "No. We all will take poison and die but I will never do this again."

Meanwhile, Shyam Lal and Lalita and their children are back to begging. Sadly, their situation has not improved by this drastic step of selling their child. The family has got ten kilograms of rice from the *panchayat* and another five kilograms of rice and one kilogram of dal from the *Anganwadi* as a kind of aid.

This case is just an example of the sorry state of our society. When the couple is already begging to survive, why do they not have the basic sense to understand that they only increase their poverty by producing more mouths to feed? Who will tell them? How will they understand this? It is in their benefit that they become parents only if they can perform their duties of parenting, that is, feed, clothe, and educate their offsprings. It is a sad commentary and a poor reflection of what our local administration, local *panchayats*, and local politicians are doing. The least they can do is to explain to such people that more children only breed poverty, ill health, and put both mother and child at risk of death. Parents have to understand that procreation is not entertainment but a responsibility of the highest order.

> **Parents have to understand that procreation is not entertainment but a responsibility of the highest order.**

Let's look at another extreme case. This is of Germany, where the reduction in population is leading to a crisis. Women there are refusing to have even one additional child, as it means more expenses and more responsibility. The government is considering offering US $15,000 at the rate of US $400 per month for the first three years of the child's life to all mothers to offset some of the expenses in bringing up a child. But not many women are willing to take up this offer. For them, good motherhood, with a secure future for their child, is more important than anything else. The women in Germany are taking their decisions because they do not want to be dependants, like the Indian mothers.

Unless the Indian women wake up, we will continue to have a population of beggars, and sell children to pay our loans.

34
Seeing Indian Women in a Time Warp

My recent visit to North America enabled me to reach out to a large group of women there, all from a particular part of India. What did I see? I saw that they were in a time warp. In fact, I felt that many of them had actually slid back in time. Instead of moving over from Indian Standard Time (IST) to Eastern Standard Time (EST), they lived in Indian Static Time (IStT). The "back home problems", which I had seen in my professional capacity which many women face, appeared to have been aggravated in USA. And they had no fallback or support systems at all.

The issues I encountered were far too many to be described here in detail. Many women came up and told me how they had to overcome broken marriages, for they had burnt their bridges behind them when they came here. They had been cheated into these marriages, to be treated as domestic servants or concubines! Demands for dowry continued unabated, with related domestic violence, topped by the alcoholic behaviour of their husbands.

To these problems have been added other problems—issues that did not exist in India for these women in particular and for Indian parents in general. These are the problems that they faced with their adolescent children who, under various outside influences, now defiantly confronted the older generation.

Youngsters have lost their identity. They really do not know where they belong. All they want is to be free to make their own choices, whether right or wrong. Parents have lost control. In fact, they are afraid to confront their own children, lest they walk out of the home.

The conflict is highest in the case of mothers who want to follow their old culture and do not want to adapt to the new environment. They do not know how to handle this defiance from their children. I was informed that many of them are heavily dependent on antidepressants.

> **Parents need to communicate with their children if they want to prevent them from getting involved in criminal activities.**

These middle-aged women have nothing left in life to look forward to, nothing to keep them busy, except perhaps either attend or organise alcohol-drenched birthday parties for their grandchildren, or keep moving to bigger houses to keep up with the Joneses.

I read a newspaper report in which a police officer of Indian origin was quoted as saying, "Dialogue and community involvement is a must to save the youth. Parents need to communicate with their children if they want to prevent them from getting involved in criminal activities.

"Parents of young teens now need to realise that they have to discuss these issues with them and not force their will on their children, because otherwise you get a backlash. . . . In essence, what I believe is that our young people do not have an identity anymore."

The news report also talked about migrant-Indian-youth criminal gangs and the problem of drug abuse. An advertisement for a de-addiction centre stated that services were available in Hindi, besides English and other languages. For me, this trip gave a lot of cause for worry.

The responsibility for allowing such situations to develop, I felt, had to be on the fathers and mothers in particular, and on the community at large, in general. In the middle of all the pressures of life, what perhaps did not get an adequate share of attention was the real education of the children on "values of life", also called "The Art of Living". In this, there is no quick fix. The role models have to be established over time.

Parents and community leaders need to lead the way. I did see some signs of a change. The debate has begun. In the meantime, a lot has been lost.

35
Where There Is a Will There Is a Way

There is an old saying—where there is a will there is a way. When such sayings are put into practice, in any appropriate form, they become examples for others to emulate. I will share with you one example which proves this.

A few years ago, fourteen serving officers of Delhi Police, of whom I was one, came together and registered a non-government organisation called Navjyoti. It was set up to eliminate crime through the methods of prevention, correction, treatment, rehabilitation, and social development. When it was registered, it was the first organisation of its kind, set up by police officers in the country, perhaps even in the world.

The traditional role of police officers is usually crime detection, arrest, interrogation, prosecution, surveillance, and intelligence collection. Police performance is judged by the number of arrests and detection of crimes and not by the level of prevention. No standard evaluation tools have been evolved for police in our country to test the level of prevention. It is certainly a lacuna in the police system, which, hopefully, will be rectified some day by visionary and committed individuals, occupying the right places in the police set-ups.

Navjyoti was born out of a commitment to treat the root of crime and its branches, and not just its deformed outcome. In order to do so, we, the police officers involved in Navjyoti, identified one major crime-breeding pocket of Delhi and initiated educational programmes there. It was a small beginning, but with such a great potential that it continued to generate its own momentum.

Today, in the huge slum of Yamuna Pushta, located opposite the Red Fort in Delhi, with a population of over 1,50,000, more than 7,000 children are participating in Navjyoti's primary and remedial education programmes.

But in order to get so many children into this school, at least the mothers had to be willing to let their children attend. In these poorest of families, each child means an income of about ₹ 50 a day, that is, ₹ 1,500 a month. This is earned by begging, garbage collection, selling plastic, child labour, diving into the Yamuna river to retrieve the coins thrown as offerings, theft, pilferage, selling drugs, and so on. Therefore, having a large family does not matter to them, in fact, it is considered profitable. The young girls, additionally, look after their siblings.

To educate such children as a part of preventive and welfare policing, Navjyoti opened *Gali Schools*, which provided education to children, with the cooperation of their mothers, fathers, or guardians. And it is this success story I want to share now.

The Navjyoti Women's Development Project implemented the concept of self help group. This involved motivating small groups of women, numbering 15 to 20, to contribute ₹ 2 to 5 every day towards collective savings. The money thus collected over a month becomes their in-house bank, to be available for loans in case of need. The women choose their own group leader. The leader and members are trained by the Navjyoti facilitators to keep records in a simple way that is easily understood by them. They hold periodic meetings, motivate other women and encourage them to help themselves in the form of a collective trade or individual entrepreneurship.

I happened to attend the first assembly of all the self help groups held at Gandhi Darshan. There were over 700 women present. Starting from none just eight months ago, there were now thirty three self help groups. Collectively, they had saved over ₹ 1,50,000. They had already opened nineteen bank accounts and twenty-one women had received loans for various purposes such as self-employment, education of their children, family health matters, and marriages of their daughters. They had put on display some of the products that they were making themselves and marketing. They were now a confident group of women, with a sense of security and purpose.

> *They were now a confident group of women, with a sense of security and purpose.*

I asked them how things had been earlier. They said that there used to be loan sharks roaming around the *basti*, offering loans. For every ₹ 1,000 that was borrowed, the lender would retain ₹ 50. Thereafter, the borrower had to return ₹ 25 every day for the next 50 days. In other words, they had to pay ₹ 1,250 for borrowing ₹ 950. The interest on the loan amounted to more than 230 percent per annum! At the same time, the lender would keep with him the borrower's *jhuggi* papers and identity card or ration card as security. The person taking the loan had to request for his ration card to be given to him for a day to buy his rations. In the event of delay in repayment, the lender would take a crowd of people to threaten, harass, abuse, or batter the borrower. At times, help from the police was also taken by the lenders to recover their loans.

"And now, what is the situation?" I asked. They said that now they only pay one rupee as service charge for the loan taken, which was also a part of their own saving.

The same women of these *jhuggis*, who had been dependent on others, are now marching forward, towards forming their own cooperatives one day.

36
Whose Fault?

I received an email from a young woman belonging to a Punjabi family from North India. Her problem is not an exception. It is happening to many others. Who is responsible? What kind of system must we have which can shame and punish these kind of persons? Can these situations be prevented?

It angers me to see what kind of society we have become. What is the point in a woman being so qualified and having so many degrees when she cannot manage issues in her life by herself? What kind of personal skills, if any, is our education system giving to our students?

Here is the email which I received, which ought to make your blood boil too, as it made mine. A few changes have been done to protect the identity of the sender.

Respected Ma'am. I'm in a great trouble and seek your help.

I am presently in a foreign country for past 15 days on a student visa. I'm a graduate in communicative English, Postgraduate in Sociology, and a B. Y.Ed. in yoga.

My father is a retired engineer. We are many children of our parents. The eldest is doing a private job and bringing up his family. I am the next one. My younger brother is a patient of a brain disease for past one-and-a-half year. He has undergone five major surgeries on brain and is almost bed-ridden and completely dependent on parents. Our youngest sister is a 23 years old widow, with two small children and ailing in-laws. Her husband died of heart attack in sleep few months ago.

I got married last year with Jasbir (name changed) of Jallandar (city name changed). He was living in Germany (country name changed) before marriage. I had met Jasbir on the internet. And we talked on phone for three years before we got married.

Jasbir showed a lot of love and care on the phone. He just won me over. The marriage date was fixed by our parents and his uncle from Germany.

Jasbir arrived in India just 15 days before marriage. Just before coming to India, he declared that he was an illegal immigrant and cannot go back. He suggested that we must go to New Zealand (country name changed) as it may be easier going there. We met only once before marriage.

Suddenly, things changed. Jasbir and his family conveyed a list of demands just two days before marriage, including 19 gold items. We had to fulfil their demands fearing their withdrawal.

But from the very first day of marriage, troubles started as my in-laws and my husband, including my sister-in-law, started taunting me for not bringing enough dowry. They often beat me up. Things worsened to such an extent that in the first 14 days of our marriage my parents had to seek the intervention of the local village sarpanch who warned my in-laws not to interfere in my life and asked my husband to take care of me.

Meanwhile, my younger brother's condition worsened to such an extent that he had to be operated upon and he slipped into coma soon after. I and my husband stayed with him in the hospital. My husband would often go to his village as well.

I went back to my in-laws after my brother recovered, and to my great shock, my in-laws did not open the door of the house, saying they have disowned me and my husband.

We were forced to leave. We hired accommodation on rent. But my husband was always in touch with his parents. He often quarrelled

> **It angers me to see what kind of society we are. What is the point in a woman being so qualified and having so many degrees when she cannot manage issues in her life by herself? What kind of personal skills, if any, is our education system giving to our students?**

with me. *Anyhow, time passed and we came to New Zealand a few weeks ago. I am here on a student visa.*

My husband abandoned me after coming here, saying he will not pay me anything for my living expenses. He left me with no money. I spent nights on roads, seeking help of the passers-by. I continued calling him on his phone, but he ignored for 8-9 days. Then he talked on phone and told me that I would never find him, he would never come back to me. He also admitted that he and his family had planned to disown me so that I may not ask for ask for any share of property.

Now I am homeless, moneyless, but in no position to tell my family about the mis-happening. I informed New Zealand police, but they are of no help. Please tell what I should do.

I wrote to her to immediately to come back home to her own country, to which she responded saying, "What will the society say? And how will my parents feel?"

Which makes me ask, "Whose fault is it if she thinks this way?" She prefers to be on the road, begging for help, than coming back. Why?

37
Use Education as a Key to Empowerment

I received a letter from an educated but disempowered woman, asking for guidance. There are common lessons to be learnt from this case. The mail has been edited for brevity and clarity.

I got married to Mr Pankaj Kumar (name changed). During the honeymoon I came to know that he was an alcoholic. At that time I only told him that it was not good for his health.

After returning to Delhi, my husband taunted me, saying I was not the type of girl he had wanted to marry as he wanted a convent educated girl. I heard it silently and did not react, to save my marriage. My husband had fully enquired about my education and family background even before the engagement.

My husband went to London and I went to my parents' home for a while and waited till he returned back to India. One day, I saw some indecent messages in his mobile which were sent by some girl called Hannah. I kept silent to avoid conflict. Then both of us went to UK.

My husband, after reaching there, told me that he was inclined to live with Hannah and if I wanted to live with him, I would have to bear this, or I was free to divorce him. After merely seven or eight days of my stay in London, my husband turned me out of the bedroom. I used to sleep on the sofa in the living room.

I also fell very ill. But my husband was not concerned. My health went on deteriorating and my condition became so critical that I was not even able to stand up. But my husband, even in such a condition, cohabited with me. My husband bluntly told me that I should go to India to my parents and get medical treatment as he did not have time for it. He finally sent me home, sick and alone. I came back and was admitted to hospital and operated. Neither my husband nor his family members ever enquired about my well being or visited me. When my condition deteriorated considerably, on repeated requests, my husband came to India. Soon, he left again for UK, without paying even a single paisa towards hospital expenses. I was left at the Almighty's mercy.

On discharge from hospital, I called my husband. He, pointblank, told me that I should leave him. He called my father and told him that he should marry me with someone else. Hearing this, my father's health started deteriorating. My husband even cancelled my return ticket to London. Finding no other option, I went to my matrimonial house, where his parents were living. I was treated very badly there.

My husband made regular telephone calls to his father, but never bothered to talk to me, even when it was my first Karva Chauth or first Diwali. In need of money for expenses, I reluctantly joined a private company for a job and also started doing MBA. I used to do all the household work every day, before leaving for my job and then on my return. My husband just did not communicate with me, even when he visited India. On the contrary, he told me to leave my MBA course and also my job. I was ready to leave my MBA course and my job. But when I asked him to give me some money every month for maintaining myself and for my medicines, he refused, saying that I was having my meals in the house and that was enough. One day, when I returned from my office, my husband, his brother, and his father closed the door of the house and refused to let me in.

I then called the police and it was after their intervention that I was allowed inside. My husband, on returning from the police station, abused me and beat me with a belt, chappals and also slapped me. He has now served me a Permanent Injunction, restraining me from entering his house.

I am now staying with my parents. What should I do? I have three younger sisters and my father is old and a paralytic patient.

After reading this mail, many questions started to crowd my mind. Why does an educated woman, who can earn for herself, chooses to be enslaved and be dependent? In this case she continued to suffer rejection to avoid going back to her parents' home, even if it meant becoming an unpaid housekeeper. Should she not have put her foot down right from day one when she found the husband a deviant, alcoholic, womanising, abusive, negligent, irresponsible, selfish, unethical, greedy, insensitive, and even violent person?

A woman's education must prepare her for all such eventualities. She must be aware of her legal rights in such situations. All these were acts of domestic violence and she was entitled to a safe house, finance, and a life of dignity. She was entitled to free legal aid and could have gone straight to a family court and sought protection.

But then, she has to know her legal rights and hate being treated as a doormat. And be willing to enforce her rights!

> *After reading this mail, many questions started to crowd my mind. Why does an educated woman, who can earn for herself, chooses to be enslaved and be dependent?*

38
Soft Backbones and Hard Hearts

Many times we are made to see certain things we may not want to. We are compelled to see them again and again because they stand out vividly to draw our attention.

I am specifically referring to the film posters outside cinema halls. Some of them are obnoxious and shameful. I recall an incident during a visit to Amritsar, my hometown. My husband, Brij Bedi, a social activist in the city, drove me around to show me the posters which had angered him. He had taken pictures with his camera to record these as evidence of public shame!

What I saw was repelling. One of the posters was of a woman sitting on the floor in her undergarments, with her legs spread out high in a V-shaped position. I was absolutely disgusted and obviously seethed with anger.

After the drive, both of us had to attend to a book release function which Brij had organised. In the audience were law students and members of the faculty, along with many senior and eminent citizens of the city.

I could not resist asking the law students what their reactions were on seeing such obscene posters. Did it not disturb them? Did they consider these as issues being beyond their control? Or was the might of the local administration too much for them? Or was it that they did not know what to do?

What was the point of being students of law if they were not learning its practical application? Along with knowledge of law, what has also to be learnt is courage and sensitivity. What is the use of education which does not instil the zeal for decency and justice? An American clergyman once asked Gandhiji what caused him the most concern. "The hardness of heart of the educated," he replied.

> *What value is the education which does not inculcate passion and fearlessness for setting right what is wrong?*

Soft backbones and hard hearts have been, and are becoming, a common feature of our world. The teacher who toughens the former and softens the latter contributes towards a worthier age. As a teacher of law, are my students learning to raise issues of injustice? Are we, as teachers, able to instil in their hearts a passion and fearlessness for truth and justice? If not, then both of them are wasting their time, the teacher and the taught, says Rajmohan Gandhi, the grandson of Mahatma Gandhi and a mentor of many in the country, in one of his articles in *Himmat Weekly*. In the case of indecent posters, all that is required is what Brij Bedi did—recorded the evidence first, and then raised a hue and cry to make it an issue of morality as well as of law.

According to the Indecent Representation of Women (Prohibition) Act 1986, indecent representation means the depiction in any manner of the figure of a woman, her form, or body, or any part in such a way as to have the effect of being indecent, or derogatory to, or denigrating women, or which is likely to deprave, corrupt, or injure the public morality or morals.

Hence, what we need to do is take a photo of these indecent posters as evidence and file a complaint with the local police. On receipt of the complaint, the local police is fully empowered to register a complaint under Section 3 of the Act, which says, "No person shall publish, or cause to be published, or arrange or take part in the publication or exhibition of any advertisement which contains indecent representation of women in any form."

The evidence of the photos themselves is substantial enough to establish the case. The content maker of the poster, the company owner, the owner of the place where it is exhibited, the publisher, all become liable.

Even though the offence is bailable, the persons concerned will become criminally liable for prosecution and face a court trial. According to the law (Section 6), the offence is punishable on the first conviction with a two-year jail sentence and fine, and up to five years jail sentence with a fine on the second or subsequent conviction. The police has the powers to search and seize all the articles involved and produce them as evidence, along with the pictures taken at the site.

It is possible that when we go to the area police to complain, it may not want to take cognisance of our complaint by saying that this is not their priority and terrorism cases are more important—this was Brij Bedi's experience—and Municipal Corporation may say this is the job of the police, when it is as much their own responsibility since the licences to exhibit posters come from them.

But as students of law and as educated and concerned citizens, we can go to the Area Magistrate and file a criminal complaint under Section 200 onwards of Criminal Procedure Code. The Area Magistrate will examine the complaint and can directly summon the accused to join the process of the trial and proceed with the matter as a complaint case. In order to get prima facie satisfaction, a preliminary enquiry can be entrusted to the police by the court. The Magistrate can even visit the site to see the situation personally.

So why keep quiet and continue to suffer? Speak up and put your learning into practice now. What value is the education which does not inculcate in one the passion and fearlessness for putting right what is wrong?

This is what learning of the law is for, with or without the fee that lawyers charge. And what better way of expressing gratitude for a highly subsidised law education in India than to take up such issues as law students?

It is sometimes said that youth is a time wasted on the young. How and when will our youth disprove this?

39
Whoever and Wherever

One question being repeatedly asked is why rapes are on the increase. Why are they happening? And why is the police not able to prevent them?

My simple response is, why will rapes not increase? What are we doing to prevent what causes rapes? What kind of young men—I do not mean all—are we producing anyway? One-third of the city of Delhi lives in slums. And if you have seen life in the slums, you can clearly see for yourself what the little children living there are likely to become when they reach adolescence.

Slums today are nurseries of delinquency, bad habits, violence, exploitation, illiteracy, unemployment, starvation for sex, depravity, prostitution, and what not. For girls, it means early motherhood, ignorant parenting, and excessive child bearing. There is rampant alcoholism, drug abuse, drug peddling, gambling at home or in the neighbourhood, and loan sharks have a huge business. Bonded labour exists there, right under our noses.

These observations of mine are not from a textbook but are based on fieldwork in the slums. These slums get the least attention from any government agency from any point of view, be it education, cleanliness, health care, employment, civic services, or crime prevention. Every inch of these sprawling slums has children loitering around, not knowing what to do the whole day. They gamble, pick garbage, sell plastic, watch adult films, indulge in sexual activities, abuse or peddle drugs, drink alcohol, eat paan, pick pockets, burgle houses, sell goods to *kabariwallas*, and collect the free food on Tuesdays from *mandirs*. No parental supervision, no school, no social controls. It is a crime-infested and crime-ridden population.

So what kind of boys will come out of these dwellings? And rapes are committed here! The rapists are here and the victims are here, but little goes reported. Whatever is reported is about the urban middle classes, who too have their own kind of nurseries incubating crime, but this large underbelly gets no media attention, for it is poor, faceless, and powerless.

> *Respect for a woman is not in isolation. It is integral to the respect for values in society and the manner in which these are treasured and translated into day-to-day behaviour.*

Also, there is an impression, which is almost a reality, within the society that girls or women will suffer and not complain due to a sense of shame, a sense of victimisation, and social taboos. Complaints also mean long trials in the courts, harassment during cross-examination, harassment of witnesses, delayed prosecution, crowded courts, with repeated adjournments and fresh dates, and so on.

While writing this article, I read a news item of how a *panchayat* in Jabalpur put a price tag for redemption for a rape case by asking the accused to pay a fine of ₹ 2,000/- and be let off. And then got sweets distributed in celebration. But the victim, this time, did not give up and went to the police and that is how the *panchayat*'s "justice" came to light.

I am personally aware of many cases when compromises were made between the parties in rape cases which were before the courts in a north-east state where I was posted. The judges themselves brought these about and let off the accused with a minor punishment. At times, they even made the rapist and the victim get married to each other. A bizarre form of justice, indeed!

From the slums to the villages to the urban areas, the educated or uneducated, how are they different? What are the youngsters exposed to? Everything, except values, which are considered out of fashion, outdated, and impractical. The directionless youth is without control and prone to extravagant expenses. It is high on tantalising entertainment, beer pubs, speed thrills, exposed to advertisements showing scantily clad men or women, and music which is almost an embarrassment, with gyrating bodies and high exposure!

Think. What kind of young men will this environment produce? For every one rapist arrested, there are many waiting on the roads, footpaths, abandoned buildings, night shelters, and prowling in cars or flashy mobikes.

Now to the question, can the police prevent these? Rape is the crime of a psychopath who is desperate for sex. He is a starved, hungry brute. For him, a woman is an object of lust. He is, therefore, on the prowl and takes his chances. In many cases the victim is known to him. He often executes the criminal act along with accomplices. He knows that he can get away. He knows the victim will not complain to the police. She will only grieve, regret, withdraw, and remain silent. And so will her family. With no one to tell what the criminal even looks like, the rapist can target his next victim without fear of being caught or prosecuted.

Arrest and prosecution in these cases requires information, identification, connecting forensic and medical evidences, and the willingness and courage by the victim to depose— and suffer the repeated dates for court hearings and cross-examination by the defence lawyers.

When society produces more Ravanas than the police can catch and the courts can punish, these real Ravanas know that Dussehra is only symbolic.

What we need today is a concerted effort to change the mindsets and make everyone respect the dignity of women.

This has to become integral to our whole way of living and thinking.

Respect for a woman is not in isolation. It is integral to the respect for values in society and the manner in which these are treasured and translated into day-to-day behaviour.

Rapes are symptoms of our overall decadence. If we want to reverse the situation, we will have to re-address ourselves, whoever we are and wherever we may be. This excludes no one.

40
Taking Care of Women in Distress

I received an email from an Indian woman married to an Indian living in the United States. Her case is not the first of its kind that I have come across. In fact, it is indicative of a deep malaise that afflicts our society and needs a coordinated response from all of us. The names have been changed to protect the identity of the person for the security and privacy of the individuals involved. I am sharing the matter with the objective of raising consciousness and encouraging a proactive response from the Indian community.

This is the email I received:

My name is Omita. I got married some time ago to Anil Bhatia, a Business Executive and a naturalised US citizen. My family identified Anil through his advertisement in a national newspaper which said, "Wanted a homely bride for a Business Executive, age 29 . . . a Hindu settled in USA. Decent family. Religion no bar." According to this advertisement, my husband was supposed to be a well-settled professional, having no financial problems, and not dependent on anybody.

When we responded to the advertisement, my husband's father visited our home and showed photographs of his entire family, including his son. After a few days, he called his son from America, and visited our home again, along with him and his other relatives. In the newspaper advertisement and also as stated by the father, we were told that the boy was working as a business executive in the US. Thereafter, they invited us to their ancestral home in Delhi.

My parents specifically mentioned to my husband and his father before the marriage itself that even though I held a professional degree, it would not be possible for me to start working in the US immediately until and unless I went through a professional course at some university in the US, and that it could be expensive. At that stage, my would-be father-in-law became furious and specifically said that after marriage I would be their responsibility and that they were capable of handling that responsibility. On this assurance, my parents agreed for my marriage.

> *Our community in US has no dearth of resources to pitch in. Together, we need to address these issues.*

On the day of the marriage, soon after I completed the signing of the marriage registration documents before the magistrate, I and my family were shocked to know that my husband was still a student, and dependent on his parents financially as he was not working. But by that time the marriage had been solemnised, therefore my parents and I chose not to make this an issue with my husband's family.

After a few days, my husband left for the US. He applied for a spouse visa. It took me more than a year to get it and I went to the US.

Initially, things were fine between my husband and I. But slowly my husband's family started troubling me. They started taunting me, throwing sarcastic remarks towards me, torturing me mentally as well as physically.

Soon, my husband also went on their side and started doing the same to me. They started to say that I was a financial burden on them and that it was a mistake on their part to have got their son married to me. So much so that my mother-in-law started saying that her sons were worth a lot of money but my parents did not realise this and did not give enough dowry.

When once I discussed with my husband that my brother was planning to buy a new vehicle in India, my husband and his family pressurised me to get money from my parents so that my husband could also buy a new car for himself. But I did not comply. I tolerated everything because I wanted to protect my marriage. I did not share these developments with my family in India lest they get mentally stressed.

In January 2004, my husband persuaded me to go back to India for a few months on the pretext that he had to study for his exams, so he was planning to shift to a hostel, and also that even I, too, could do some professional course in India, as I could not do any studies here. Though I was reluctant, he got me a return ticket and I came to India.

But soon I received summons from a US court for the dissolution of our marriage. I was absolutely shocked and surprised at this sudden turn of events. My family and I had done everything we could have done, both individually and financially, to ensure that my husband and my in-laws were satisfied. Like, for instance, on all festivals and occasions generous gifts were given. But all this was in vain, it appears. They expected much more.

I am leaving for the US now to defend my case there, but I am going alone, unsupported, with no idea about any legal procedures. Please, I request you to advise me about how I should pursue my case and also about any good lawyers, NGOs, and women's organisations in the US. Also, please suggest if there is a way that I can file a case on them from India against the fraud and torture that they have committed towards me. Would really appreciate if you could please help me get justice.

Omita is already in the US to fight back, but without sufficient resources. But the point is that these situations are far too many these days. We need well-publicised and credible contact points, maybe through our Indian NGOs or the Consulates, to let the young women know how to get help in case of need from their own Indian Missions, or the NGOs so identified. The Indian Missions then, in partnership with the NGOs, could do the referrals. With this, our women, at least those who need help outside their own country, will not be homeless or feel abandoned.

Our community in US has no dearth of resources to pitch in. Together, we need to address these issues.

41
Are They Pretty Pageants or Beauty Contests?

Why not call beauty contests pretty pageants? This question was asked by a young man on the NDTV 24x7 programme *The Big Fight*, which I watched on the internet when I was in the US. This question sent me researching and exploring. I will share with you my findings a little later.

The arguments put forward by the exponents, for and against, on the issue of beauty pageants were both very engaging as well as diametrically opposite to each other. This is what attracted my attention.

First were the arguments in favour of these beauty contests. The contests are an exercise of freedom of choice. They are legal, they don't break any law. They are also a form of entertainment. They have been there for the last forty years. Hence, there is a demand for them. They are not about the body, but rather the in-depth exercise in someone's future development. They are body plus looks. They are a complete personality package of those who can handle stress, passion, and charity work. They are all about a functioning democracy and the right of women to make choices and women are mature enough to make these. What is wrong with seeking upward mobility by the participants? They give women the flexibility to wear what they want to wear. They are about the choice of a profession. They are about empowering women and opening more windows of opportunity for them. They are about mutual agreement to promote a product. The products anyway had to come, for the world is a global village, so it's all in step. This is the way that society has moved. Society gets what it deserves. Those who have a problem need not go watch them.

Now the arguments against these contests. They are all about the larger social implications concerning the way the women are treated and exploited in society. They are all about beauty types. They are all about body sizes. They are sexist. They are "a piece of money". They are about selling creams. They are a meat market. They are used to promote an artificial beauty criteria. They promote anorexia in the way they display the woman's body. The idea was developed in 1921 to keep the tourists at the Atlantic City beach resorts. How many women can be five feet nine inches tall? They are selling an unreal dream, which sets high expectations and challenges, leading to complications for women in general. Beauty cannot be categorised in terms of 36-24-36. You cannot judge a personality by two questions. Page Three has now made it to Page One. A quicker way to get noticed. They are all about becoming "artificial jackets". They are all about looks. Otherwise, why are the dark-skinned girls with snub noses and thick lips from Africa not selected?

I went to the thesaurus to understand the question as to why we cannot call these contests pretty pageants. I consulted Roget's International Thesaurus, a book that brings together in one place all the terms associated with a single thought or concept.

I found the following words associated with the term *beauty*: prettiness, handsomeness, comeliness, gorgeousness, sight for sore eyes, masterpiece, glamour girl, doll, adornment, attractive, charm, elegance, bloom, glow, charisma, daintiness, thing of beauty, make-up, cosmetics, beauty-care products, pancake make-up, talcum powder, foundation, lipstick, nail polish, cold cream, perfume, shampoo, vanity case, shapeliness, good looks. . . . This list is not exhaustive.

I searched for linkages to intelligence, intellect, and brains. But these were not found associated with the word *beauty*.

Why were we getting agitated and wishing for something that is not in the meaning of the word *beauty* in the English language? In a beauty contest, the focus is only on looks and appearance and all that goes to enhance them. It is a business like any other. And a huge global business, worth billions of dollars!

> *In a beauty contest, the focus is only on good looks and all that goes to enhance them. It is a business like any other.*

This is, of course, not a judgement on the issue but an analysis of the question posed during the programme, which was intended, perhaps, to find a deeper meaning of the word *beauty* and substitute it by another word *pretty*. But, as is evident, both these words are synonymous. Hence, there appears to be a need to locate a word that may meet the requirements of those who would like to give a deeper meaning to the word *beauty* by offering the concept of a beautiful brain in a beautiful person.

42
Danger Zone: Men and Women at Work

I was watching a CNN programme on fidelity. I did not go away in the middle. I watched the entire programme, for it appeared very authentic in its analysis, giving very studied facts. The anchor of the programme was candid in stating that, in the US, one out of every two marriages suffered from infidelity. In other words, 50 percent of all marriages suffered from the "other man" or the "other woman" factor.

And what is of equal concern is that the women are catching up. Workplaces are now being labelled as Danger Zone: Men and Women at Work! This is also called the Coffee Cup Syndrome because 62 percent of all love affairs, according to the survey, started at the workplace. It starts with "come-ons" to common deadlines or work pressures, to the sharing of secrets.

Everyone is considered vulnerable, even though fidelity is the core of marriage. Monogamy is more a myth and an exception, and adultery is the rule in 50 percent of all divorces. In fact, the judges are now asking, "What, besides adultery?"

Even though 90 percent of the people say that it is wrong, yet there is evidence of a huge proliferation of "cheating hearts".

What are the recognised traits of a cheating husband? He stays late at work. He looks forward to excessive travel and does not complain about it. He hopes not to get caught. He tries to follow the fifty-mile rule, which is keeping the person with whom he is having an affair at least fifty miles away.

And if caught, he just denies and denies it and keeps telling himself that he can get away with it.

> *The challenge of marriage does not end with the marriage vows but, in fact, begins with it.*

For women, most of these affairs start as friendships, which lead to unintentional love affairs. The relationships remove loneliness, to start with. The women receive attention, affection, compliments, and get to hear all the nice things they want to hear. They go out together with their companions for drinks, meet at secret rendezvous which, in most, cases result into being all over each other.

The survey further revealed how the internet has fast become an electronic bedroom. It's also called a "sexual smart book". People with polygamous propensities will always find someone to indulge in "sex chat" on the internet. Easy access to pornography and excessive indulgence in it has become the cause of two-thirds of all divorces, as reported. They were all cases of "crossing a line on line".

An attempt was made to study if this kind of cheating was in our genes. And the answer was, Yes! Animals, too, cheat all the time. Only one species was detected to be monogamous—the flat worm, which lives in the intestines of the fish!

Hence, monogamy is a myth in the animal kingdom. It was found to be rare and did not come naturally. The fact is that infidelity is imprinted in our psyche. Females are polygamous for resources and the men for spreading their genes.

But this did not mean that, for humankind, acting on impulses is inevitable. Are we so much unaware all the time? Are we slaves to our animal instincts to such a great extent? If so, then what is the intellect for? What is the discerning power in humankind for?

What is most needed is education, the experts said. But what kind of education are we talking about, I wondered. And where and by whom will it be imparted?

The challenge of marriage does not end with the marriage vows but, in fact, starts with it.

In the West, and equally elsewhere, there is a need to undertake an introspection on these vital issues affecting humankind more and more each day.

Any message for us Indians?

43
Will They Listen to Me?

This fortnight was full of creative happenings for me, from which I drew a great deal of learning and inspiration. The happenings which I am referring to were:
a) Presence of Muslim women in a training programme.
b) An interaction with over 120 officers, men and women, of one of our country's premier civil services.
c) The release of a police manual on gender issues for police trainers.

In all the three events, the common thread happened to be women at different levels of development in our society.

Let me come first to the Muslim women.

I was one of the speakers at the closing session of a training programme for Muslim women, sponsored by a trust and supported by large hearted Muslim donors and an overseas bank. It was a heartening experience to see that the Muslim women's needs, too, were slowly coming in focus. I heard some of their feedback and saw what a huge difference it had made in the attitudes of these women after they had gone through the training. Perhaps it was a first such exposure for them!

Many of these women were sitting in the training room with veils on their faces, while I was there among them in my police uniform. They listened to me with great respect and awe.

I wondered how much more time they would take to shed these "curtains" from their faces. I wanted to ask them that if the men decided, would they still continue to stay behind their veils? How much was it the men's decision and how much was it theirs? Or was it faith based, as they believed?

Well, this was India with all its diversity and opportunities. But I was quite surprised to see that the Self Help Group (SHG) programme for women was still alien to them, when it has become such a success in micro-credit schemes for women all over the country. This programme had been specially mentioned and supported by our Finance Minister in this year's budget speech.

Apparently, these women watched television more for entertainment than knowledge and information. I told them that, while such training programmes are of immense importance, today the media has educational value too, if they choose and watch suitable programmes. It only depends on the viewer's choice.

But this is one large segment of Indian society which truly needs the special attention of the government and the non-government sector.

In the question-and-answer session that followed, one of the answers which was probably difficult for them to accept was when they wanted to know about work-home balance. They asked me, "What has made work and home possible for you?" I replied, "Small family size."

For most of the women sitting in the audience, this was still not an achievable dream. Limiting family size was not in their control. Ironically, this was a real problem for many women decades ago.

But these women are not the only ones unsure of themselves! I got to see this when I went to speak to probationers of a premier civil service of our country. After I finished my speech, one of the women officers who accompanied me to my car asked me, "Madam how will my juniors take me if I assert myself? Or if I make a mistake? Or if I tell them not to do a particular thing in the manner they are used to doing? Will they listen to me as a woman?"

I replied immediately, "Of course they will! A lot depends on how prepared you are, how well trained you are. And how well informed you are. And how confident you are. And, certainly, how willing you are to learn even from your juniors, knowing that they could have more knowledge than you, especially initially."

She had qualified for the premier civil service of this country. Yet she was not sure of herself and had many doubts.

She went back, wondering about the tough and long professional journey that lay ahead of her, more so as a woman. She was not in a veil. She had qualified for the premier civil service of this country. Yet she was not sure of herself and had many doubts. I wondered was she an isolated case. No, she was certainly not! Most women professionals have the same questions.

Now on to the third issue: a matter of training men in the police force to respond and enforce matters which concern women's safety and security. I was invited to present a critique on the training manual being released for Police Trainers.

The training manual had been brought out by the Centre for Social Science Research, Delhi. I found it to be very useful. It had excellent material for police trainers to help them train the police trainees on gender issues, particularly domestic violence and trafficking in women. But the pertinent question I asked was—while the trainers have this material to train, who are the trainers and what is their background and motivation?

So far, training in police is still not a matter of priority. Those appointed to the training unit feel discounted since they have been assigned less important responsibilities. Unless police training becomes a priority for police leadership, well written manuals like these will remain unutilised.

In fact, if the police training policies all the states all over the country are collected and compiled, it may be an eye opener for everyone. Some states may still not have a well-defined training policy! Delhi Police itself did not have one till just a few years ago.

So much for fighting terrorism, naxalites, communal riots, and crimes against women!

Is anyone listening? Being sidelined or "not being heard" has to reduce.

44
Women in Uniform: Who Are They?

This article is not about percentages or a head count of women in uniform but *who* these young women in uniform are. And what made them opt for olive greens, khakis, blues, the jungle fatigues, or the naval whites? And what they could do with what they get into!

This article is also an attempt to examine what kind of work culture these determined and inspired women get to work in. Is it what they had anticipated or envisioned? Or is it a surprise or a rude shock to them? How do they deal with what they get into? Equally, how does the organisational culture accept, impact, tolerate, conflict, imbibe, respect, or reject them? Do they feel fulfilled, trapped, disillusioned, or shattered? Do they just reconcile themselves to the situation?

Do these women entrants team up in the male-dominated and male-controlled uniformed services, which they undoubtedly are? Or do some of them dare to carve out their own paths? Or do some get isolated, maladjusted and, perhaps feel out of place? How do their juniors, peers, managers, and leaders deal with the gender differences, which are a fact of life, and get to work with them? Does the organisation leaves them on their own or are they assisted, groomed, mentored, or empowered? Is there any written or agreed policy that the uniformed services must necessarily create an environment of smooth absorption, acceptance, respect, and growth for them so that the organisations continue to attract more women in uniform?

The source of all my questions are the different situations I have encountered in one form or the other.

Women, today, who are opting to join uniformed services, are not doing so due to a whim or a fancy. They are also not being persuaded by others. They are there because they want to be there. It was their dream to be there, immaterial of rank or kind of service. It was their intense desire to be in uniform and become somebody. It can be for serving the nation, or their own professional expression and growth.

These women entering uniformed services are aware of the hardships which come along. They are conscious of the fact that the profession they are joining is not an ordinary one. They are aware that the work involves tenacity, endurance, risk, and willpower. The work also means moving to different postings at different locations and being away from the family. At the same time, they also expect and believe that with these costs and sacrifices, they will realise their potential and be a source of pride to their family and friends. Most of all, they will be self-empowered and exceptional achievers.

Women who opt to join the uniformed services are already meritorious, strong-willed and focused in what they want to do and want to be. They are selected on merit. At the time of entry they go through and pass the same tests as those prescribed for men.

And the organisations want them for compelling reasons. They are needed, as is said, because the services to be provided to the society as a whole need their perspective. Or else the service will not serve the interests of everyone completely.

But take the case of police services. Even when policing is for the society as a whole, and in many cases it involves additional focus on women's issues, women police officers comprise an abysmally low percentage in the field, policy-making, training, and decision making. Even the few who are in service are marginalised and are poorly visible. This applies to all ranks. This is not because there are no suitably qualified and competent women to fit the requirements, but even when they are, they are not identified, deployed, groomed, trained, selected, or appointed.

The fact is that while a section of women are ready to take on the challenges, the organisations recruiting them are still not ready. They are still in a time-warped and led by old, hierarchical mindsets which are patronising and are protective of their domains. Their attitudes still go back to men being providers—caring and commanding, brothers and fathers. Or husbands who take all the decisions.

It will take quite a while for this generation to alter and change their mindsets. The true test will be to see what changes a woman will make once she is at the helm. This is a situation which is being feared, I suspect, today. Women in uniform will, predictably, get there, but right now they are far away!

> *Indian institutions, particularly uniformed services, are still not prepared to be led by women. Hence the onus is on women of calibre and will to make new inroads and be the trailblazers all the way.*

I personally trained many young women in police, along with the men. The women were comparatively more committed to serve. Regrettably, hardly any of them are visible on the streets—be it patrolling, investigating, directing traffic, frisking, or escorting. They are, more often, seen as duty officers in juvenile bureaus, missing children squads, or are running welfare centres. Basically, all matters predominantly concerning women and children are allotted to them, but not much beyond.

Women who enter these professions are looking for wider and bigger challenges, but are restricted to traditional gender roles, even when they can do much more. Many times, by the time they are "gifted" an opportunity to perform the traditional male roles, it is too late for them. Their skills are not up-to-date, their families have become demanding, and even they prefer to opt out for fear of failure. They do not fail but are progressively driven to it. They were not groomed when they were young, hungry for growth, and excited to take on challenges.

The women come with energy and expectations of exciting work when they enter service. But they lose the enthusiasm by force of circumstances. They are then seen to settle down, hopefully, with whatever comes their way. Exceptions become Sushmitas—the one who recently committed suicide.

Meanwhile, these women in uniform, who had been trained and are no less than others, are left unequal in exposure, experience, and generic and specialised skills. The society and the nation do not reap the benefit of the contributions which they have the potential to provide.

Behind a successful man in uniform has usually been his wife. Behind a successful woman in uniform has often not been her husband, but her own family—of course there are exceptions!

Indian institutions, particularly uniformed services, are still not prepared to be led by women. Hence the onus is on women of calibre and will to make new inroads and be the trailblazers all the way.

They must not wait!

45
Unjust God?

Has God not been unjust to women by entrusting the biological functions of giving birth to humankind without arming them with all the necessary and essential resources? I wonder, was it on purpose? To keep the woman dependent, restricted, and subjugated?

One of the first direct consequence of motherhood, be it at the beginning or later, is the impact on health. At the same time there is restricted mobility. Then is the responsibility of nurturing the child till he is grown up enough to take care of himself and become independent.

I was a speaker at a very well-attended seminar organised by the Indian Medical Association and Jan Uday, an NGO. In fact, I was pleasantly surprised to see such a big attendance of men, besides, of course, the women whose case the seminar was pleading. Professionals, comprising nutrition experts, gynaecologists, psychologists, and sociologists listed out the challenges of overseeing the special needs of prospective and expectant mothers and in bringing up the children.

From the research data presented by the experts, it was evident that nature had been unjust to women to a great extent. And certainly towards those innumerable women who are left to fend for themselves in such a state—before, during, and after motherhood—be it rich or poor. And India has millions of them!

It is sheer agony and pain, especially for a poor or a lonely woman, to bear children when there may be really no one who cares and understands what she goes through once she is pregnant. An expectant mother, especially in such circumstances, as informed by the experts who preceded me, suffers from innumerable inadequacies. Some of the important ones which impact her the most are:

a) Accidental and frequent pregnancies over which she literally had little or no control.

b) In most cases she does not even understand what it means to be pregnant. The impregnating man, hopefully a husband, is rarely bothered to see whether the prospective mother is mentally and physically prepared to be one.

c) Absence of a relative or close friend who may be oriented or interested in providing her the support to understand pregnancy.

d) The expectant mother just goes through the nine months of pregnancy, hoping that all will be well. And that in the end she will be gifted by a son.

e) Most serious is when she goes in for a child hoping it will correct a deviant father—I have seen many such cases at our Navjyoti Family Counselling centres.

I believe that two of the most important social responsibilities are being a public representative and being a parent. Unfortunately, people with these responsibilities do not receive any serious training, or even prior counselling for their responsibilities ahead. There is no known training or counselling service for them either. Their responsibilities are not recognised as disciplines to be learnt in a college, even though there is no doubt about the enormous contribution they make towards the future of the society and the nation.

Young couples wanting to become parents are, at times, totally ignorant of what being a parent means. The prospective mother is even more clueless. At times, for months, she does not even know that she is pregnant. I have known a case of a woman who was six months pregnant and had no idea that she was expecting her second child. She thought she was merely putting on weight.

The husbands, too, are ignorant or indifferent as to how they should support their wives carrying their child. During delivery, fathers are nowhere near. They are even afraid to hold their newborn child in their arms. They are not present during delivery to realise how extremely painful it was for the mother to deliver.

> *While the law of nature is irreversible, the state of affairs in our society can be reversed.*

How much of her goes into nurturing during and after the pregnancy is immeasurable. But only the mother knows this. All her own nutrition goes to her child while delivering and feeding. And there is usually nothing extra left for her.

So her body ages many times, while the man is the same, ready and almost waiting to demand the next child. The poorly spaced children are born weaker and impoverished. The woman, like livestock, at times aborts or delivers one baby after another, without her body getting much time to recuperate.

I wonder, at times, what if nature or God had given the capability of bearing children to men. Would the men have died during childbirth? Would they have been malnourished? Would the women have been missing at the time of delivery by their wives? Would men have lost work or given it up? And would they have gone on to have so many children and make our country's population over a billion? And would they have accepted domestic violence for not delivering the preferred gender? And would then women have been raped?

This is how one's heart can cry out when confronted with ground realities of the voiceless women! While the law of nature is irreversible, the state of affairs in our society can be reversed. The solution lies in giving all humankind a sensitive and a grateful heart.

It is obvious that God needs to do some more homework!

46
India's Emerging Face

Last week I was asked to express my views on the woman of today and challenges before her. This is what I said:

The Indian woman of today, across the country, is gradually becoming different from the one I saw when I was growing up and preparing to join the ranks of the government. Most of my friends, at that time, were getting ready, by themselves or after being told by their parents, for marriage. All their attendance of school or college was only a preparation for being married into a well-off family.

Marriage, to my friends, meant a life long security with both the man and his family, who would give them a safe, well-provided, and hopefully a happy home, with a number of children, preferably sons. The parents were busy matchmaking, saving, and preparing for their daughters' marriages. Dowry was on display. I saw many such exhibits—the gold ornaments, the silver, saris, and expensive gifts for all the relatives. This made a large impact on me and made me rebel against it all.

While all this still exists in many different dimensions, in all sections of our society, a lot has, thankfully, changed for the better.

I now see parents of girls very keen to see that their daughters become financially independent about their own needs. They are preparing their girls to beat the dowry menace and the insecurities of marriage. The teachers are educating the girl students to stand up for themselves. They are making them conscious of their potential. The graduate and postgraduate courses are now becoming need-based vocational degrees. The educational institutions are conducting special awareness programmes to make girls stronger. The media is playing an important part in raising awareness. It has placed women's issues forcefully on the agenda. The courts,

> *Motherhood, too, is becoming more planned, with small family the norm.*

the law enforcement agencies, and the law-makers are under a continuous scanner on women's issues. And there are so many women focussed non-government agencies with a lot of capability and resources to deliver on their objectives.

In the media, creative writing has become substantially richer. Look at the women's magazines, women authors, pages dedicated to women's issues in national dailies, and so on. It has all changed for the better. Women journalists in print and visual media dominate and even crowd the scene.

Women themselves have changed and continue to find their own place by their own merit. My visits to schools and colleges clearly reveal this. Today's girl has become conscious of her capabilities and strengths. She is asking questions. Why can she not be what she wants to? Or achieve success like her role models?

Today's women are aware women. They are no longer prepared to be told what to do. They know what they want. They are highly motivated and work hard to achieve their goals. They identify their goals and chase their dreams.

The range of opportunities for them are as never before. There is no profession beyond their capability or reach. They have seen it for themselves. They are qualifying for these positions by their own merit and not due patronage or favours. They are also proving to be the new face of the country.

These new women are looking at marriage not only for security, but also for friendship and companionship, while protecting their own space to grow. They are rejecting and also questioning the dominance of the man or the family, unlike the mindset earlier.

No wonder, two things are happening. One, increased break-ups of marriages. For most women, there is certainly a reduced tolerance for indignity or assault on their self-esteem, when they feel as such. Second, marriage for such kind of women is no more mandatory to make a position in the society. This means that late or no marriage is a viable option. Motherhood, too, is becoming more planned, with small family the norm.

This is the new Indian woman. The onus now is equally on this class of women, especially the privileged ones, to craft and energise a new India, which imbibes the best of the past and the present, and help the country to become a superpower of "humanity", full of values, which also provides enough for all and especially for the less privileged.

47
National Rainbows

Last fortnight I met three national rainbows, that is, three outstanding women of our country—two in Kutch, Gujarat, and one in Pune, Maharashtra. All three women are self-made, born of strong visionary mothers and fathers—though Lila Poonawala lost her father when she was only two, are industrious, extremely generous, sensitive, and visionary. I look at them as representatives of the countless, invisible women who are as brave and dedicated. This article is a salute to them on this Independence Day. I call these three women our national rainbows.

Right now I am writing about only one of the three. I cannot compress the contributions of all three in just one article. I will write about the other two at some other time.

This article is about Lila Poonawala.

I was invited by Lila, ten years ago, for the inaugural merit scholarship award, financed from her own hard earned wealth. The first one to receive the scholarship, out of a batch of ten girls, was a twenty-year-old, Neetu Bhatia. Neetu went on to do India proud when she became a student of Franco Modigliani, the Nobel laureate in economics, and also assisted him in his work and research papers. She works at Harris Nesbitt, the US Investment banking arm of Bank of Montreal. Her title is Vice President, Media, Communications and Technology Investment Banking.

I had told Lila that I would return for the ten-year celebrations, if they happen. We kept the date!

This time, ten years later, I saw the impact of her visionary spirit. Lila had reached out to more than 300 girls, with nearly seventy of them studying in prestigious universities in India and around the world. Except for a few like Neetu, the majority of the recipients were from absolutely marginalised sections of the society. The fellowships were for as varied subjects as could be—computational genomics, radar and landsat thematic mapper images, research in environmental factors for Alzheimer disease, breast cancer, and NASA related technologies, to name just a few. These girls are called "Lila Fellows".

This time I was curious and wanted to know Lila a little better. And I learnt some interesting things about her.

The India-Pakistan partition in 1947 rendered Lila's family homeless and they had to flee to India from their home in Sindh. The two-year-old toddler, along with her mother and siblings, found herself at a refugee camp and, a few months later, at a modest house in central Pune.

Lila started going to a municipal school and later moved to Mount Carmel School. She developed an interest in Mathematics and Physics and also in extracurricular activities like NCC, scouts and guides, hockey, cricket, badminton, and even gliding!

It was her mother who emphasised to Lila the importance of independence. Her interest in science increased and she developed a passion for technology. In 1967 Lila became the first woman mechanical engineer in Pune. She joined Ruston and Hornsby as a trainee. On the first day of work, she met her future husband, Firoz, who would be the strength behind her. Ten months later, she moved to Vulcan Laval, a Sweden headquartered multinational company.

It was on the shop-floor of this engineering company that her professional journey began in earnest. Times were changing and this was very apparent during the sixties. While working women could be seen in many areas, it was still uncommon for a woman to be part of a hard core engineering company. But nothing dampened Lila's enthusiasm.

She was appointed as Exports Manager in 1978. Those days were the days of the "License Raj" and industries needed licenses to import. The government would give some cash incentives on exports. Vulcan Laval needed both, the licences for imports and the cash incentives for exports.

> *It was her mother who emphasised to Lila the importance of independence.*

Export procedures were long, cumbersome, and required extensive documentation. It would take months to get approvals from the bureaucracy.

Though frustrating at times, Lila never gave up. She had a tremendous ability to deal with people and drive a hard bargain. She succeeded in winning many customers and taking the modest exports of Vulcan Laval to unprecedented heights.

A deal for ₹ 280 million with the USSR and the success of this project brought her to the forefront. Here, she got the opportunity to show her managerial skills. This brought her to the notice of the senior management and she was promoted to the position of General Manager, exports and marketing.

During this period she had done various courses from IMM, the Indian Institute of Management at Ahmedabad, and Harvard and Stanford Universities in the USA.

In 1986, she was appointed as an Executive Vice President. This was also the year when she appeared on the cover of the international business magazine *Svensk Export*. It was a unique honour. It was the first time a woman from the corporate world in India was featured on the cover of an international business magazine of repute.

With an excellent track record to back her, she was appointed the Managing Director of Vulcan Laval in 1987. With this appointment, she became the first Indian woman to be appointed as managing director of a multinational company in India. She also became the first woman in the Alfa

Laval group globally to reach that position. She remained the only woman managing director in the entire group until her retirement.

Under her leadership, the company moved from strength to strength.

Lila had the foresight to see the potential and the growth of business in the food sector. She laid an emphasis on research and development in the company. In 1993, King Carl Gustaf XVI of Sweden inaugurated a state-of-the-art Alfa Laval Technology Centre in Pune. This centre was built to provide essential research and development facilities. It was her vision to set up world-class research facilities in India and make India an exporter of world-class products.

Lila got the Padma Shri award in 1989, another first for a woman from the corporate sector in India. The King of Sweden conferred the Royal Order of the Polar Star on her in 2003.

It was Lila's earnest desire all along to do something substantial for the girl child. Her dream got an impetus on the 16 September 1994, on her fiftieth birthday. Her company, Alfa Laval, wanted to reward her for her outstanding performance with an expensive gift. She suggested them to give her a cash reward instead. The company gave her a birthday present of 100,000 Swiss Francs. It is with this and her own savings collected over the years, that she launched her dream project — Lila Poonawala Foundation.

Today, Lila has supported over 300 worthy and the brightest daughters of India, who are spread out all over the world, as "Lila fellows". They all adore their mother-mentor. Never mind if Lila and Feroz do not have biological children of their own.

A salute to the Lila's of India.

Jai Hind.

48
Two Interesting Experiences

I was a guest speaker at the Founder's day celebrations of Lady Irwin College, known for its prestigious home science graduate courses, besides many others. While the annual report was being read by the Principal, I went through the college brochure. It triggered my thinking.

Some naughty thoughts started to trickle into my head. As I got jotting them down, Mrs Gursharan Kaur, wife of our honourable prime minister and the chief guest of the function, asked me if I was preparing my speech. I said, "In a way yes." My mind had got charged with some interesting ideas. I told her I would be teasing the audience and the college a little in my speech. Even while I was still collecting my thoughts, I was called up to speak.

This is what I said.

I asked the audience, comprising the faculty and the students, that since this college was a premier home science college of the country for girls, how would it be if we had a home science college exclusively for the boys? There was an instant laughter. I wondered, would the boys have sought admission if such a college existed? Would it have been as popular a course as it is for women? And what difference would it have made in these male students in their approach to various issues of life?

The emerging trend among working women is that marriage is an additional work for them and why should they get stuck this extra work? Beyond companionship, marriages are a lot of work with large responsibilities. Well-placed career women are no more seeking financial security or a roof on their head through marriage. They have them from their own resources. They only want intelligent companionship and trusting friendship. They do not want the traditional patriarchal control of a husband who demands care and nurturing similar to the kind he received traditionally from his mother.

I further posited, would studying of home science by men make a difference to their mindsets? Would they make better companions for career women?

My second teaser was, what if the marriage advertisements have parents asking for grooms who are educated in home science?

My third teaser was, if it was not time we gave a new name to home science. The whole subject of home science had gone beyond the boundaries of home. I received a large applause on this, which meant that this was what all the students also wanted, but obviously had not been successful!

I suggested that we let the ideas of what the new name could be come from the students. This was endorsed by the prime minister's wife, too, in her speech. She said that the time had come to find another name for home science.

I also observed that we had been insensitive towards male education. The society has actually kept men away from many avenues where their sensitivity could be increased. And then we complain that they are not as sensitive as we would like to them to be!

Now for another experience. While driving down to attend the annual function of a school, I got talking with the teacher who was in the car with me. She had been teaching for eighteen years. I asked her what the most visible changes were which she had seen in the students over the years.

The biggest change, she said, was awareness. The children of today are much more aware of what is around them. Besides this, respect towards elders has declined considerably. The children are becoming adults a little too soon. Parents do not spend enough quality time with their children because of their own priorities. Children today prefer indoor instead of outdoor activities.

> *What if marriage advertisements have parents asking for grooms who are educated in home science?*

I asked her, "Do you, as teachers, attend training programmes to address the changing environment? Should we not accept certain matters now as realities so that we focus on what can be done rather than what is out of our hands? We should try to be better prepared."

She said, "No, we do not train for this. It's more on each of us how we handle these changes. But it would definitely help if we assess and upgrade our skills at regular intervals."

Then I asked her, "Do you, as teachers—and parents also—come together to communicate or share trends or observations beyond the PTA (parents teachers association) meetings on what parents must know about the children? And do parents also share with teachers what they have to say concerning their children's studies or any other matter which the teacher needs to know?" She said, "No."

At this time we arrived at the function and our conversation ended.

But it was not the end. For me this was a matter of great concern. Why do we not think through such simple problems for solutions? They cost nothing. But left unattended they certainly cost the nation a lot!

No Shot Cuts

I was invited this week by the Students' Union of a well known university from the so called "cow belt" to give a talk. It was a very different invitation from the ones I usually receive from academic institutions. The difference was subject of the talk: "Criminalisation of Student Politics". Usually, students' unions do not pick up such a thorny subject, that too in a university and a state which is known for criminalisation of politics itself, not just student politics. Therefore, it was a pleasant surprise and merited proper respect.

As I entered the university hall, I saw that it was packed to capacity, but full of boys mostly. There were very few girls present. I enquired if the university was only for boys. I was told this was an indicator of the culture of the university. Girls avoided events where boys were expected to turn up in large numbers.

Then I realised why I was also slated to have an exclusive session with the girls after the main event. I was told that the girls felt shy to ask questions in the presence of the boys, hence they avoid coming to listen to such events.

I thought that was tragic! I was glad I had accepted the invitation to give the talk and took the opportunity to give them all a sugar-coated strong dose. The best part was that they took it in silence and with respect.

First about the dose or experience with the boys and then the girls.

The introductions began with a large number of student representatives and union members, present and past, coming on to the stage to present big, fat garlands to me. There were far too many garlands for my height and weight! Obviously, it was a situation where the organisers had to accommodate or oblige everyone for the photo opportunity.

Those who came up on the stage waited till the photographer had clicked their picture. I was told that a few of those presenting me the flowers had been on the wrong side of the law. I, obviously, was in no position to select or stop them. But I did not allow a re-circulation of the presented garlands, which often happens in such events. I kept with me the ones given.

> *There are no short cuts to building confidence or life-skills for anyone, whoever it may be.*

But the fact that the past and present union leaders came to hear what I had to say, knowing that what I was likely to say may not be very pleasant for them, was indicative of the positive pressure they had come under. Basically, it had become an increasing need for acceptability and respectability, whatever the past may have been.

I began by asking the boys present in the hall if they, as students and as youth of this great university, individually and collectively, had a plan? I explained that just as the country has an economic plan, a political plan, an educational plan, a defence plan, and now a disaster management plan, what was their plan? And should a university or a college not have a collective plan, a collective dream, a collective vision? What was their mission statement? Could any of those present stand up and tell me?

The truth is, I said, that from the silence to my question, we can say that most of the youth merely drift. And is this not a possible reason for some of the young men to become mere numbers in a crowd, to be used by others—to demonstrate, bully, or attack? "Those of you who have a focus and a plan cannot be used or abused," I asserted.

Criminalisation in universities happens when some students are on "sale" and when education is not their focus. Cheap recognition or popularity is their immediate motive. These "bought" students know they will not make it in the examinations, hence they choose mentors who may get them a degree without deserving it. They are lured by false assurances, expectations, pretences, and money. That is why they are on sale in the first place. Students who do not have a focused plan for their student career have their time on sale, for cash or kind.

The criminal elements are in need of such "fools". These people come hunting and entice young, gullible minds to fall into their traps. The new recruits get into the records of the police and intelligence agencies and thereafter have to "buy" their certificates of good antecedents. Once they cannot get a clean verification, they find it safer to stay in the criminal sanctuary. This is how criminalisation gets rooted.

The presence of these criminals fouls the academic atmosphere of the university. While serious students struggle with exams, the criminalised elements try to put off the exams for the flimsiest of reasons.

I then concluded, "So who fixes this minority which causes so much harm? The majority—which is you!"

Now on to the interaction with girls. One look at them gave away the question written large on their faces. They all wanted to know how could they continue and study further when their parents were not encouraging them to do so.

A very tough question to answer! And what do I tell them? The girls were there only for a degree, not for a career. Only very few had their parents blessings to move on and build their careers. For the rest, they were there just for the sake of the paper-degree, to be married as soon as they finished their course. They were all birds, getting ready to be flown out to a new nest. They pleaded with me to tell them what to do.

During this time, I had noticed that the girl who was with

me was literally trembling when she had introduced me. I asked her if this was her first stage experience. She said yes, it was. I asked the girls what was the stage here in their hostel for? For others? Why not them? Why didn't they take turns daily and go on the stage, to find within themselves their hidden, unexpressed talents? This would be one of the strongest ways by which they could acquire confidence and learn to stand up for themselves. And confidence was what they were lacking most. I turned to the teachers present there and requested that they assist girl students to do so. I also suggested that the university should hold some sessions with the girls' parents at regular intervals.

There are no short cuts to building confidence or life-skills for anyone, whoever it may be.

50
Questions Which Need Answers

One morning, a young woman in her early twenties came to my residence and left a handwritten note with my wireless operator, which raised certain questions. The note was in Hindi, and I have translated it.

She wrote: Is a woman born to grow up and live only according to the rules set by men and the society? In our country, a girl is taught from day one that she is not to go by what she thinks and feels is right, but by the directions and orders of the men or the elders. If they order her to stand, she should stand; if they order her to sit, she should sit. She is also destined to marry only the person her elders choose. A society in which girls are treated like cattle to be given away, can neither progress nor survive too long.

At the end of the note, she said that she would come to my residence at 9 a.m. the next day to speak to me. And she did. As I came out of my house, I saw her waiting impatiently for me. I was in a rush to leave to attend a meeting I had committed earlier. But she would not let me go. She started to raise many sensitive questions which needed a lot of time to answer.

I told her I would get back. But I also told my assistant at the residential office to connect her to our Navjyoti counsellor. I sensed that she wanted her visit to be kept confidential and off the record.

I had her handwritten note with me and I started to read it in my car. As I finished reading it, I called up my residential office from my mobile phone to talk to her and counsel her not to be desperate, which she evidently was. I was worried that she might harm herself. I was also afraid she might go away and not come back, for she had wanted to remain anonymous.

I asked her on the phone to tell me what was really wrong. She said, "I want to study and do my MA, but my family is arranging to marry me off, which I do not want." I asked her, "Why don't you check out what kind of proposal your elders are considering? Check out if they would be interested in your continuing your studies after marriage." She replied, "No, I cannot consider anyone now because I have already accepted another man to be my husband." I said, "This, then, is your real problem—your emotional acceptance of another man whom your family will not accept." She had no firm answer. She also said that if her parents came to know that she had met me for this reason, they would lock her up and perhaps even do away with her, as had been done with a few girls of her village.

> *The real problem today is that women want security with growth, mobility, and challenge, but the parents want only security for them.*

The following weekend I happened to be in a workshop on parenting, organised by a well known Delhi counsellor, Dr Aruna Broota. I shared this case with the participants there and suggested we analyse what went wrong.

Parenting means not just conception, giving birth, feeding, clothing, educating, and getting the daughters married. It is the whole preparation and development of a life we give birth to. And in our society, as also elsewhere, the most untrained act and duty each one of us performs is of becoming a parent.

There is neither a concept of, nor adequate access to, premarital or post-marital counselling so that mistakes can be prevented, as far as possible, by parents and young couples. Such a programme is now being implemented in

Singapore, where it is mandatory for all young couples to take a counselling session before marriage. It would be worthwhile to see how and what they are doing and with what results.

But our country is so big. It is urban-rural, rich-poor, educated-illiterate, forward looking-backward, with palaces and slums. All coexist. Where do we begin then? And who foots the bill of counselling and training?

The fact is that there will remain a large difference between need and availability. The problems of the kind I have mentioned are already huge and numerous. In fact, they are an issue in almost every Indian home, in one form or the other. The consequences are there to be seen in many forms, including an increase in the number of call girls and also in the increase in the number of cases of molestations of girls.

So where do we go from here? The real problem today is that women want security with growth, mobility, and challenge, but the parents want only security for them. When we educate a girl, how can we tell her not to think for herself? She needs to be heard, listened to, explained to, reasoned with. Neither the parents nor the children are not completely wrong, but parents need to understand the changes which have come with education, media awareness, and access to opportunities.

Therefore, training of parents is very essential. In many homes today, bringing up adolescents and living in extended families is one big hell. We need to face the problems upfront and prepare to prevent breakdowns and agonies of the kind I have shared here. The young girl's case referred to is an example of the widespread problems in many homes.

There are answers. We need to seek them and use them.

51
Women as Catalysts for Transformation

The subject of discussion for the conference was "Women as Catalysts for India's Transformation." It had only women as speakers and I was one of them. Fortunately for me, I was the last one, which helped me get some time to listen to the earlier ones and collect my own thoughts on the subject. As I heard the passionate and experienced speakers, many questions started to rise within me, and then the answers, too, started coming in.

I was in a five-star environment and the audience comprised women from higher income groups and also the educated and professional classes. They were evidently confident, self-assured, and seeking more to progress in life.

As I observed them responding to the earlier speakers, I sensed the direction in which we could move to raise our contributions in a manner which becomes truly transformative. It was in this direction that my mind started to race, to ask myself certain questions, which had hidden answers.

My subconscious probably had the clues, but right then what were surfacing were question marks.

Let me share with you the questions which came to my mind on how women could, if they were to, become catalysts for transformation.

Q: Is there a transformation in the way the educated and the professional women of today are bringing up and supporting their families, as they are now equal bread earners and also work outside their homes, like the men?

They are now at par with men in professional skills and even salary or income—I am talking of the class which falls in this category.

Q: Is there a difference in the way women work, for they are now employers too and are also the direct bosses?

Q: In what way has the integrity levels in the general administration gone up, if at all, with the presence of women?

Q: Is there a difference in the way women are dressing, in view of their mobility and time pressures?

Q: What is the difference in their purchasing styles?

Q: How do women view money and savings in view of their economic independence?

Q: What kind of bosses are women making?

Q: What kind of colleagues or peers are women?

Q: What kind of quality lives are women leading now?

Q: In what way are they differently visible?

Q: In what way are they impacting the younger ones? Are mothers becoming role models for their children?

Q: Are women leaders offering better and transformational leadership? Is there any style emerging? Is there any particular style typical for women professionals?

Q: Are they offering more options and creative alternatives?

Q: In public perception, are women emerging as better, preferred, as compared to men, or more credible persons, officials, organisers, and so on?

My questions were that if we women believe, or the society expects, women to emerge as a transformative class, then how are we making a difference for the better? Has the emergence of educated women improved the quality of life in the sections of society where they interact? For example, the work place, home management, policy making, or the way we do business, or run the government? Or the way women are bonding? Or the way they are organising themselves? Or the way women are looking at larger responsibilities as citizens?

Each question is a topic of research and analysis. We need to get answers to all these questions, for we need to know about the real situation.

> *Women, as a new class of leaders, can play a critical, transformational role in the society.*

For instance, the contribution which the women *panchayat* members have made in the village which elected them: Have they done better? If so, why? If not, why? Has it been transformative or merely transactional?

The fact of the matter and the reason for asking all these questions is that women, as a class, are the new hope. Expectations from them are different in many respects. Are they aware of this yet another responsibility on them? How do they become aware of these expectations? By self-awareness or through outsiders?

One observation which I want to convey through this article is that women, as a new class of leaders, can play a critical transformational role in the society, provided they become conscious of the prevailing (wrong) practices in governance, professional management, and personal relationships. They need to resolve to reject them individually and collectively. Only then, I believe, women will emerge as catalysts of transformation for a new India, on the way to be better led on all fronts—home, neighbourhoods, communities, work places and of the society as a whole.

Women—Educated but Still Disempowered

Women's empowerment is one subject that been endlessly discussed and debated in numerous forums, especially in a plethora of conferences, seminars, workshops, as well as in the electronic and print media, and also in a large number of books and other publications. One may wonder as to what more can be said on this issue.

Consequently, in this chapter, I have decided to turn the topic on its head. I will focus here on "women's *disempowerment*"! I will highlight some situations in which women have become considerably disempowered–willingly or unwillingly. Women tend to succumb to such situations and weaken their own position. I will also identify some of the traditions, practices, behaviour patterns, and circumstances which disempower a woman instantly or over a period of time. I will mention some of my own experiences to show how I ensured and sustained my own empowerment, essentially by *refusing to get disempowered*, irrespective of the odds stacked against me, both in my personal life as well as in my professional activities. And I would like to emphasise that constant vigil is absolutely necessary to maintain empowerment; a woman should not lower her guard at any point of time. In this discussion, I will confine myself to women in Indian.

Undoubtedly, in many situations, a woman is disempowered by circumstances beyond her control, but in many others she becomes disempowered by her own actions, since she does not realise their short or long-term impact.

Such disempowerment is even more surprising in the case of "educated" and "professional" women, who we normally consider "empowered".

Let us embark on a journey in the life of a woman. Let us start with her birth.

Well, none of us gets to choose our parents. We just get them; even the adopted children have no choice in this matter. Such is the fact of life. It is my belief that empowerment or disempowerment of every child, more so of a girl, begins at birth and depends on the parents the child is born to. In the case of a girl, if the parents welcome her birth and she receives all the love and care they can give, she begins her life with empowerment. If there is a congenial atmosphere at home and she gets adequate nourishment and rest, she is on the road to empowerment. But if she is born into a family in which she is unwanted because she is a girl, as happens so often in India, she starts her life with disempowerment, *for no fault of hers*. She begins with a serious handicap, which has a cascading negative effect during the vital, formative years of her life, a time when, in fact, she needs all the support and help she can get. In India, unfortunately, a large number of women belong to this disempowered category.

> *Every child, girl or a boy, is born with (potential) wings to soar in life, but if no one teaches them how to fly, they remain grounded.*

The next level of empowerment depends on the school the girl child goes to. Hardly any child chooses her own school, it is the parents and guardians who do so. Therefore, the sort of educational opportunities she is provided, in school as well as in college and beyond, apart from extra-curricular activities such as sports, cultural, and literary pursuits, build her foundation or corrode it. During her growing years, every single passing day strengthens or weakens her, as the case may be, before she enters adulthood.

Every child, girl or a boy, is born with (potential) wings to soar in life, but if no one teaches them how to fly, they remain grounded. A boy, somehow or the other, manages to learn that he is supposed to be self-reliant, but a girl may or may not learn the same lesson. In case she does not, she remains dependent on, or is influenced by, her immediate family members or her circle of friends, unless, by her own efforts, she manages to break free. In most cases, the girl grows up, attuned to disempowerment, at times knowing well that her wings have been clipped because she is a girl. Such girls invariably become helpless and are unable to take decisions, even minor ones, on their own. The girls belonging to this category grow up and become disempowered women because of circumstances over which they have almost no control.

Exceptions are occasionally there. For instance, when a teenager refuses to get married as she is still a child and rejects the child-husband. How she gets that inner spark, nature alone knows!

During the course of my community work over the decades, I have come across many women, victims of circumstances, leading lives marked by deprivation, uncertainty, and inadequacy and who are subjected to all kinds of harassment, including physical violence and sexual exploitation. Such women give in meekly and reconcile themselves to their destiny or surrender their freedom to their "captors", until, by some twist of fate, say, getting motivated through community programmes organised by NGOs, their disempowerment is reduced, at least to some extent—if they become fully empowered, it would be a miracle! You can find examples of such instances in my book *What Went Wrong and Why* (Hay House Publishers India, New Delhi, 2012).

Now let us consider the case of those women who have been born into caring homes, have acquired good educational qualifications including professional degrees, and have begun earning, but who disempower themselves despite all the opportunities and advantages they have gained. I have met many such women who have slid from empowerment to disempowerment.

Let me give an example. The slide usually begins with a woman's marriage and carries on thereafter. When an educated—and even an economically independent—woman agrees to marry someone not of her choice under pressure or into a family that demands a huge dowry, which could include expensive items such as a luxury car, from her parents and who also insist on an ostentatious marriage, with all the accompanying ceremonies, including expensive gifts for all and sundry, she takes the first step towards disempowering herself.

During the wedding, the fact that she is forced to go through outdated rituals clearly sends out the message that her position is subordinate to that of others, including her parents, her husband, and in-laws. For instance, I would like to mention that the custom of *kanya daan*, in which the bride is formally "given away" to the groom by the girl's parents, represents an educated woman, but still disempowered, as if she was a commodity. This custom implies that the husband-to-be is hereafter her "protector" and she is in his "custody". She invariably gives up her economic independence to be acceptable to him. I wonder why there is no *purush daan* applied to men!

Post-marriage, she gives up her dream of achieving something substantial in her career or life and accepts her husband's and in-laws' commands. She also readily agrees to change her surname and sometimes even her first name on the insistence of the family she is marrying into. She succumbs to pressure to become a mother without really wanting to, and goes for sex determination of the foetus, although it is illegal, under compulsion. If the foetus is female, she could even be forced into an abortion. She is compelled to ask her parents to fulfil her in-laws' "requests" on social occasions or festivals. These "requests" could range from money to costly presents. She keeps a one-sided fast during *karva chauth* for the long life of her husband, while there is no such reciprocal ritual for her husband. She starts depending entirely on her husband for all her personal needs as she is forced to hand over her salary to him, in case she is working. As a consequence, she is regularly insulted, rebuked, and even physically harmed. Under threat to her or her family members, she is forced not to press charges of assault against her husband or in-laws. She is also forced to apologise to them in order to maintain harmony. As a result, the woman disempowers herself almost completely. The fact is that she weakens her own position considerably through her own actions or inactions and concedes her equal status over a period of time.

A son is considered the natural inheritor of the family assets, whereas the daughter is not. The son automatically acquires the family business and property, including all assets like the house, jewellery, or antiques. The family does not expect the daughter to take the family legacy forward, except in rare cases. Later on, at any stage, if she stakes a claim to the family assets and wants to be an equal partner in the family business, she has to assert herself forcefully and may even have to resort to legal measures.

Let me recount how I guarded myself against disempowerment. Even as a student, I did not blindly accept the subjects offered to me in my favourite school. They gave me subjects like home science just because I was not good at arithmetic. As I was keen on studying science along with a language of my choice, I walked out of this school and joined another one that gave me the subjects I wanted. My parents fully supported my decision, even if it meant leaving the best school of the city. I chose universities that awarded me scholarships based on my merit.

I chose a life-partner who would not hold me back and who was willing to encourage me to soar professionally. We married as two equals. As a couple, we jointly paid for the reception after a simple marriage ceremony in a temple. I did not rush to work in the kitchen just because I was a daughter-in-law and was supposed to do it. I continued visiting my parents and dropping my sister at her school by scooter, as I used to do earlier. I did not keep any one-sided fasts. I continued playing tennis and won several trophies. I was fully committed to my job in the Indian Police Service.

In other words, post-marriage, I did not change my lifestyle. I was married, but that did not mean I was not a daughter too. I offered to hire a domestic help and a cook for my mother-in-law, out of respect for her, if she would accept them. I was grateful for the jewellery gifted to me by my mother-in-law, but I returned it, respectfully. I bore only one child, a daughter, as that was all I could possibly manage, keeping in mind the pressing demands of my profession and resource constraints. I obtained the support of all my family members by opening up my home, equally, for my in-laws, parents, and the rest of my family, while keeping full control over my own income and securing myself financially. I dressed according to the situation so that no distraction was caused at the work place. Inappropriate dressing also leads to disempowerment in its own subtle way. A woman cannot possibly wear a swimsuit to office!

> *The positive aspect about empowerment is that an empowered woman can empower others at the same time.*

Finally, I would like to emphasise that, at several stages in the life of a woman, she becomes vulnerable and her situation could be exploited by those with evil intentions or nefarious designs. Empowerment requires being constantly on guard and equipped with a strong shield to prevent being made a victim.

A woman's life can be exceedingly versatile and enriching for society if she is empowered. On the other hand, if disempowered, she becomes a liability for herself and her family, at times, without her realising it. Empowerment is something to be consciously learnt and constantly practised so that it becomes a part of a woman's nature. It is a lifelong process.

The positive aspect about empowerment is that an empowered woman can empower many others at the same time. Empowerment is the capability to say *yes* to what a woman believes in and to say *no* to what she does not believe in. The absence of such capability is disempowerment. Every woman should try and acquire this capability, even when faced with adverse circumstances.

My message to all women is simple: *Remain empowered. Because you are worth it.*

(This article has also been published in the author's book *Dare to Do*)